MEN OF THE 65TH

The Borinqueneers of the Korean War

TALIA AIKENS-NUÑEZ

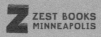

ZEST BOOKS
MINNEAPOLIS

*For Tata. Thank you for telling me the story of the
Borinqueneers. Your story. Rest in Peace.*

Text copyright © 2023 by Talia Aikens-Nuñez

Zest Books™
An imprint of Lerner Publishing Group, Inc.
241 First Avenue North
Minneapolis, MN 55401 USA

For reading levels and more information, look up this title at www.lernerbooks.com.
Visit us at zestbooks.net. 🖪 🖾

Designed by Athena Currier
Cover Illustration by Leo Trinidad

Main body text set in Adobe Garamond Pro.
Typeface provided by Adobe Systems.

Library of Congress Cataloging-in-Publication Data

Names: Aikens-Nuñez, Talia, author.
Title: Men of the 65th : the Borinqueneers of the Korean War / Talia Aikens-Nuñez.
Other titles: Men of the Sixty Fifth : the Borinqueneers of the Korean War
Description: Minneapolis : Zest Books, [2023] | Includes bibliographical references and index. |
    Audience: Ages 11–18 | Audience: Grades 7–9 | Summary: "Learn about Puerto Rico's 65th
    Regiment, one of the US Army's most decorated regiments. Author Talia Aikens-Nuñez
    shares the history of these soldiers and the discrimination they faced as they served their
    country during the largest court martial of the Korean War"— Provided by publisher.
Identifiers: LCCN 2022023596 (print) | LCCN 2022023597 (ebook) | ISBN 9781728449623
    (library binding) | ISBN 9781728479149 (paperback) | ISBN 9781728486017 (ebook)
Subjects: LCSH: United States. Army. Infantry Regiment, 65th—History—Juvenile literature. |
    Korean War, 1950–1953—Regimental histories—United States—Juvenile literature. |
    Korean War, 1950–1953—Participation, Puerto Rican—Juvenile literature.
Classification: LCC DS919 .A354 2023 (print) | LCC DS919 (ebook) | DDC 951.904/24—
    dc23/eng/20220525

LC record available at https://lccn.loc.gov/2022023596
LC ebook record available at https://lccn.loc.gov/2022023597

Manufactured in the United States of America
1-50432-49941-11/29/2022

CONTENTS

FOREWORD

On June 10, 2014, President Barack Obama signed an Act of Congress awarding the Congressional Gold Medal, the highest civilian (non-military) award bestowed by the United States government, to the US Army's 65th Infantry Regiment, also known as the Borinqueneers, for their service during the Korean War. The 65th Infantry Regiment was the first segregated Latino military unit and the first unit of the Korean War to receive such a distinction. In awarding the medal, Congress recognized the bravery and heroism with which the Puerto Rican soldiers of the regiment served their country. Only four US Army units have received the Congressional Gold Medal.

The United States Army's 65th Infantry Regiment is perhaps one of the most unique formations to ever fight on behalf of the United States. Consisting of Puerto Ricans both white and Black, the unit was formed shortly after the end of the Spanish-American War of 1898 to police the island. These soldiers did so well that the unit grew into the Puerto Rico Battalion (of about one thousand men) and then the Puerto Rico Regiment (of about four thousand men). That regiment later became the 65th Infantry Regiment of the United States Army. Serving in the United States Army became a matter of pride for many Puerto Ricans, with fathers and brothers serving together before, during, and after World War II (1939–1945).

The 65th Infantry's most challenging moment came after North Korea's invasion of South Korea on June 25, 1950. When the regiment arrived in Korea, it was the largest and best trained in the US Army. By law, all the regiment's soldiers and sergeants (called noncommissioned officers or NCOs) were Puerto Rican. Most of the officers were white or continental (meaning from the United States). In 1950 white and Black soldiers served in different units of the American army. But in the 65th Infantry Regiment, white and Black Puerto Rican soldiers served together. It was the only unit in which this was the case.

In Korea, Puerto Rican soldiers battled well-trained North Korean and Chinese soldiers. They did so while struggling through the terribly cold winters, marching up and down very steep mountains, and wading across wide rivers. They also had to fight against discrimination and prejudice. Some US officers and soldiers believed the smaller and darker-skinned Puerto Ricans could never be good soldiers. But the men of the 65th Infantry Regiment proved them wrong. Thrown into battle again and again, they gained the respect of not only most American soldiers but even the North Korean and Chinese soldiers they fought against. General Douglas MacArthur, who commanded the US-led United Nations forces during the war, wrote of their ability and courage, and of his pride in having them in his command. The Borinqueneers stayed in Korea for more than three years. Too many died. Too many were wounded.

I once asked a Puerto Rican soldier why he fought in Korea for the United States that sometimes didn't treat him very well. He just smiled at me with no hard feelings in his heart and said, "Because we were American soldiers from Puerto Rico. It was what was expected of us. And what we expected of each other and ourselves."

Gilberto Villahermosa
Colonel, US Army (Retired)
August 27, 2022

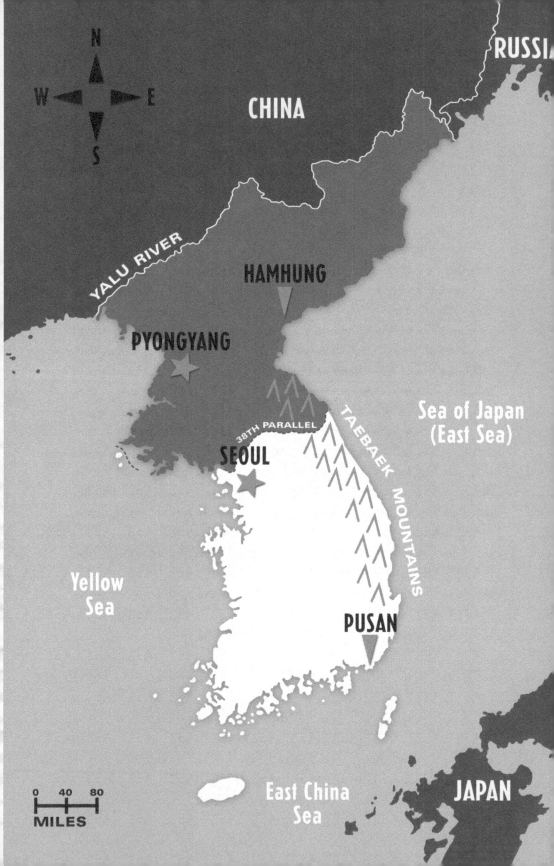

INTRODUCTION
Valor or Betrayal?

Bullets whizzed by as Sergeant Modesto Cartagena's platoon climbed Hill 206. The earth under their feet rumbled with the impact of grenades landing around them. With so much dust and dirt in the cool air, the sun could barely poke through the haze. As the platoon climbed the hill, Cartagena saw his fellow soldiers falling under the intense machine-gun fire of the Chinese forces on the hill above them. But Cartagena kept climbing.

It was April 19, 1951, nearly a year since the United States had entered the Korean War (1950–1953). The jeeps and tanks of Puerto Rico's 65th Infantry Regiment had just arrived near Yeongcheon, South Korea, with orders to take a strategic enemy fortification known as Hill 206. But the Chinese People's Volunteer Army (PVA), which had entered the war the previous year to assist North Korea's losing forces, did not give up ground easily. Hill 206 was no different.

A shot rang out from the hill above, and Cartagena felt his machine gun jerk. He looked down and saw that it had been hit by a bullet. He hadn't been shot, but his gun was broken and useless. He knew his platoon couldn't continue under this assault. He had an idea.

Cartagena charged up the mountain, ignoring the sounds of intense enemy gunfire and the explosions of grenades around him. He lobbed one of his own grenades over the piles of earth and sandbags ahead of him and into the enemy's first emplacement.

BOOM! The grenade detonated, destroying the enemy's store of weapons and killing the enemy soldiers protecting them.

Cartagena turned to the rest of his platoon down the hill behind him. He shouted for the men to stay in cover. He turned and ran up the hill by himself. Enemy grenades rained down around him with loud blasts of earth and shrapnel. Dirt rained down everywhere. Cartagena grabbed enemy grenades thrown at him. He quickly pitched them back at the enemy. He saw the enemy soldiers ahead of him duck for cover. While they hid, Cartagena quickly ran up the hill toward them. Throwing a second grenade and ducking for cover, he destroyed a second emplacement.

Cartagena didn't have time to catch his breath. Soon he was knocked to the ground by a nearby enemy grenade. But he shook himself off, got up, and charged the next emplacement. He destroyed five emplacements before a torrential downpour of grenades landed around him, stopping him momentarily in his tracks. The grenades exploded, knocking him flat on his back. But he got back on his feet again and again. Lobbing grenades. Shooting at enemy soldiers as they rose from their emplacements. Blood poured from a wound, staining his uniform.

Finally, his platoon was able to rush to his side. They rushed Cartagena and the other wounded soldiers to the first-aid station as the fighting continued. He had lost a lot of blood, but he had saved his platoon and pushed the enemy back. Soon the 65th Infantry Regiment took Hill 206.

Nine days later, another soldier of the 65th Infantry Regiment showed extraordinary heroism by risking his life to protect his fellow soldiers. The 65th had moved to meet PVA forces near Kalma-Eri, south of Hamhung. Master Sergeant Juan E. Negrón took a vulnerable position on his company's right flank after the enemy had overrun a

Many decades after the end of the Korean War, Sergeant Modesto Cartagena (*second from the left*) was among the veterans of the 65th Infantry Regiment honored at a ceremony at the US Army Reserve Center in Puerto Nuevo, Puerto Rico. He was one of the most highly decorated soldiers of the war.

section of the line. The company was ordered to withdraw, but Negrón refused to leave his position. He remained to defend the withdrawal of his fellow soldiers, firing at the enemy troops who had broken through the roadblock ahead. As the enemy forces closed in on his position, he began to throw grenades, halting their progress. He held the enemy through the night until allies could launch a counterattack, providing him with the cover he needed to finally withdraw. When he got up, exhausted, there were fifteen enemy soldiers lying dead only a few feet from his position.

Cartagena's and Negrón's stories are only two of many about the heroic acts of the 65th Infantry Regiment during the Korean War. The 65th, also known as the Borinqueneers (pronounced *bor-ehn-kin-EERS*), was the biggest, longest-standing Latino military unit in US history and the only one that remains on active duty. The regiment had served in both World Wars with distinction before being sent to fight in the Korean War, during which it received nine Distinguished Service Crosses, 256 Silver Stars, and 606 Bronze Stars.

So the US public was shocked to discover that during the war, 162 soldiers of the 65th Infantry Regiment had been court-martialed and ninety-one of those soldiers found guilty of disobeying orders and desertion.

The US military kept the courts-martial quiet. But the soldiers of the 65th sent letters to their families describing what was happening, which led to a public outcry and confusion from the press. How could one of the most distinguished regiments of the Korean War, whose soldiers had only months before been praised by General Douglas MacArthur for their "brilliant record of heroism," become involved in the largest mass court-martial of the Korean War?

Did the Borinqueneers lose their bravery and heroism in such a short time? Or were they victims of discrimination in a prejudiced and segregated system? Were they betrayed by the country they risked their lives for?

This is the story of one of the bravest and most decorated regiments in the history of the US military. It is a forgotten story in a forgotten war. But it is a story of patriotism, loyalty, and bravery in the face of danger and discrimination, and it is one that deserves to be told.

CHAPTER 1
Puerto Rico's Regiment

The 65th participated in many roles but [were] always used as laborers or for security missions, not for fighting [before the Korean War]. The military did not want to use them because the military still operated from the premise that non-whites cannot be [soldiers] or perform as well as white soldiers.

—Harry Franqui-Rivera

The story of the Borinqueneers begins in 1899, after the United States gained Puerto Rico as a territory and Congress approved the creation of a group of volunteer soldiers from Puerto Rico called the Puerto Rican Battalion of Volunteer Infantry. Puerto Rico had been a part of the Spanish Empire for over four hundred years until the end of the Spanish-American War (1898), in which the United States supported Spanish colonies' revolts against the Spanish Empire. The United States swiftly defeated Spain in naval battles, and the war ended with the signing of the Treaty of Paris in August 1898, which placed Puerto Rico under US control. The name of the island was changed to Porto Rico,

Naming the Land

When Christopher Columbus landed on Puerto Rico on November 19, 1493, and began the process of colonization, people already lived on the island. Columbus called them the Taíno Indians. The Taíno lived on multiple islands in the Caribbean Sea and Florida, including Puerto Rico. They called the island Boriken or Borinquen (Land of the Great Lords). Columbus called the island San Juan Bautista in honor of St. John the Baptist. Over time, traders and sailors called the island Puerto Rico ("rich port" in Spanish). Some Puerto Rican towns still have their Taíno names, such as Mayagüez, Utuado, and Humacao.

and in 1908, Congress passed an act changing the name of the volunteer battalion to the Porto Rico Regiment of Infantry. It wouldn't be until 1932 that Congress changed the island's name back to the correct Spanish Puerto Rico.

Just after the Spanish-American War, people born in Puerto Rico were not citizens of the United States. To become part of the US Army, they had to take the oath of US citizenship, take a new officers' oath to serve in the military, and pass a tough physical test. The new volunteer battalion created a path for Puerto Ricans to become US citizens.

In 1917 President Woodrow Wilson signed the Jones-Shafroth Act into law. This gave US citizenship to anyone born in Puerto Rico after April 25, 1898, near the start of the Spanish-American War. The law also required Puerto Rican citizens to enter the military draft, requiring them to join the military when the country was at war and if the government called on them to fight. The US has not had a draft since 1973, but before that men were drafted for many wars in US history.

The Father of the Guard

Major General Luis Raul Esteves was born in Aguadilla, Puerto Rico, on April 30, 1893. His father was in the Spanish military and encouraged Esteves to enter the military. Esteves graduated from West Point, the United States Military Academy, in 1915 alongside young soldiers who later became Generals James Van Fleet, Omar Bradley, Joseph McNarney, and Dwight Eisenhower (later the thirty-fourth president). While at the academy, Esteves was the Spanish tutor to Eisenhower. Esteves was the first Puerto Rican to graduate from West Point.

Esteves was an instructor of officers in the Porto Rico Regiment of Infantry at Camp Las Casas. He is widely considered to be the "father" of the Puerto Rican National Guard. The National Guard protects the island through military and civilian missions as well as prepares soldiers if a war arises. He organized and led training camps around Puerto Rico for Puerto Rican officers. He died in Puerto Rico in 1958.

It didn't take long for the Porto Rico Regiment of Infantry to make a name for themselves. On March 21, 1915, two years before the US officially entered World War I (1914–1918), the *Odenwald*, an armed German ship carrying supplies for other German boats in the Atlantic Ocean, attempted to exit San Juan Bay by force and without clearance papers.

The Porto Rico Regiment of Infantry was stationed in El Morro Castle in Old San Juan under the command of Lieutenant Colonel Teófilo Marxuach. Marxuach gave the order to fire a warning shot at the *Odenwald*. Sergeant Encarnación Correa fired a machine gun mounted on the walls of El Morro Castle at the ship, but the *Odenwald* ignored the shots.

Marxuach then fired another warning shot, this time from a cannon on the castle wall. Recognizing the seriousness of the situation, the

Odenwald stopped in its tracks. It was forced to return to port, where the ship surrendered to the United States and its supplies were confiscated. Marxuach's shot is considered by some to be the first shot fired by the United States against the German forces during World War I.

The US officially entered World War I in 1917 after the Germans sank several US ships and tried to persuade Mexico to attack the United States via a telegram that the British intercepted. In May the Porto Rico Regiment of Infantry recruited nearly two thousand men who were immediately sent to help defend the Panama Canal, a newly built artificial channel of water that separated North America from South America and provided a crucial trade route for ships passing from the Atlantic to the Pacific Ocean.

At the time, the United States mandated racial segregation, requiring soldiers of different races to serve in separate groups. The military

The Porto Rico Regiment of Infantry, circa 1906. Teófilo Marxuach is fifth from the left in the top row.

falsely believed that white soldiers performed better than non-white soldiers, so white troops served in combat roles. White officers would also often lead units of non-white soldiers.

This kind of segregation was not practiced in Puerto Rico, and Puerto Rican soldiers often refused to label or separate themselves by skin color. But because of racial segregation and discrimination policies in the US military, the regiment was limited to support and security roles during World War I.

Despite this limitation, the regiment returned home to Puerto Rico in 1919 as heroes. By June 1920, the unit had been fully integrated into the US military and its name was changed from Porto Rico Regiment of Infantry to the 65th Infantry Regiment.

Twenty-one years later, on December 7, 1941, the Japanese Empire conducted a surprise attack on the US naval port of Pearl Harbor in what was then the US territory of Hawai'i, and the next day attacked three other US-held territories: Guam, Wake Island, and the Philippines. The shock of this attack removed any question of the United States entering World War II. Congress quickly moved to officially declare war against the Japanese Empire the following day. Once again, the United States was at war.

Old Fortress

The Spanish built El Castillo San Felipe del Morro, also called El Morro, in the 1500s. Located at the edge of Old San Juan for soldiers to watch and guard San Juan Bay, El Morro is a large castle. The grand structure was an active military base during World War I and World War II. El Morro has become a national park where families picnic on the grassy field or fly kites. Every day, people tour all six levels of the old fort to see the cannons, living quarters, prison cells, and main plaza where troops would gather.

Territorial Claims

During the Spanish-American War, the United States needed strategic positioning in the Pacific Ocean. The United States annexed Hawai'i in 1898 to use the naval base at Pearl Harbor. It became a US territory in 1900. As a territory, Hawai'i was not given voting members in Congress and could not elect its own governor or judges, so the people on the island had little power. Some of the island's residents tried numerous times to become a state so that they could have the same rights as other states, while others sought complete political independence from the US. All those efforts failed. Many scholars believe this was due to their large non-white population. After the attack on Pearl Harbor in 1941, ushering the United States into World War II, numerous bills were presented in Congress to make Hawai'i a state. Finally, in March 1959, Congress passed a bill granting statehood to Hawai'i.

The Japanese Empire was part of the Axis powers, an alliance of countries that included Nazi Germany and the Kingdom of Italy. Japan had joined the war for many reasons, but a major one was to gain land for the empire. Many European countries held colonial territories in Southeast Asia that the Japanese Empire wanted to control. The surprise attack on Pearl Harbor was meant to destroy the United States' naval presence and leave Japan free to take US-held territories in the Pacific Ocean. But it backfired, because the attacks galvanized the US public to join a war that many in the US had originally wanted to keep out of. By declaring war on Japan, the United States joined the Allied forces. It included global powers such as Britain, France, and the Soviet Union (a union of fifteen republics that included Russia).

Because the 65th Infantry Regiment was part of the US Army, they were already trained for battle. But this was going to be a major conflict, and so the regiment began even more extensive military training in 1942. They were trained in working with ammunition and in difficult physical exercises at camps in Tortuguero, Cayey, and Salinas and at Fort Buchanan in San Juan.

The US military still enforced segregation during World War II by separating non-white soldiers into their own units commanded by white officers. During an interview years later, retired Staff Sergeant Gabriel Soto-Rivera remembered his surprise from when he was asked during basic training to remove his shirt and show his skin. "That's how they determined to which unit the black Puerto Ricans and the white Puerto Ricans would go. Well, I was surprised because we, Puerto Ricans, have always interacted with [one another] just the same. I was kind of embarrassed by it. That's where I learned that there was racism in the Army."

Just as in World War I, the 65th Infantry Regiment, like other predominantly non-white units, was barred from combat roles and limited mainly to support and security missions due to racial prejudice. After their training, they were sent to Panama again to defend the Panama Canal and the Pacific and Atlantic coasts.

But their time guarding the canal wasn't long. Soon they were needed elsewhere. In January 1944, the men of the 65th traveled by boat to New Orleans, Louisiana, for further training before being sent east across the Atlantic for the first time to fight in Italy and North Africa.

When they arrived in Casablanca, Morocco, the 65th Infantry Regiment continued their training, this time in amphibious assaults, and served in security missions. While in North Africa, Colonel Antulio Segarra took command of the 65th Infantry Regiment. He was the first Puerto Rican officer to command a regiment in the US Army.

Later that year, the 65th Infantry Regiment was separated. One battalion went to France to protect the army headquarters from German land or air attack. Another battalion conducted security missions guarding trains that carried war supplies and fuel to Allied outposts, while the third battalion went to the Maritime Alps region to guard the France-Italy border.

The soldiers stationed on the France-Italy border were ordered to keep watch to see if the German army would try to attack southern France from Italy. The conditions in the Maritime Alps, surrounded by high snowy mountains, were cold and wet. They were very different from the tropical climate of Puerto Rico or the dry and hot Mediterranean climate of North Africa. One soldier, José Blas García, later recalled going without a bath or shower for a month. He developed an infection in his hand that sent him to the hospital. While there, he received antibiotics and lived off what little food was available, mainly hot dogs and water. Other soldiers developed trench foot, a very painful condition that affects the feet when they are wet for long periods, causing them to swell and leaving them vulnerable to infection. Gonzalo Villanueva was one such soldier. He spent ninety days guarding the 1,600-foot (488 m) mountains without taking his shoes off. When he and other soldiers were coming down, he was barely able to walk. They had to cut his shoes off because his feet were so swollen.

The 65th Infantry Regiment finally entered combat in December 1944, when German soldiers attacked the battalion in the Maritime Alps. Seven men from the 65th Infantry Regiment were killed in skirmishes with German forces that December, and another ten were wounded.

In the spring of 1945, the men of the 65th Infantry Regiment reunited and were moved to Lorraine, France, to help the Allied forces. The US Army had halted the advances of the German troops and was pushing farther into Europe. In March 1945, the 65th Infantry Regiment crossed the Rhine River into Germany alongside the rest of the US Army. It was the beginning of the end. By early May 1945, Germany had surrendered, ending the war in Europe.

Soldiers of the 65th Infantry Regiment rest and replenish their energy after a full day of practicing maneuvers at Salinas, Puerto Rico, before shipping out to the Panama Canal.

The 92nd Infantry Division was a segregated division composed of Black soldiers and commanded by white officers. During World War II, it was the only division of Black soldiers that participated in combat.

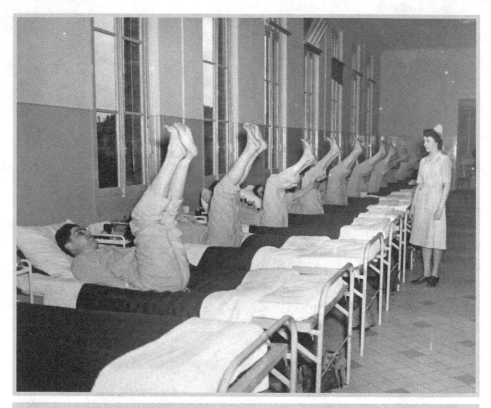

An army nurse supervises soldiers suffering from trench foot as they do exercises to help alleviate their symptoms and heal.

After the war, the United States, Britain, and France occupied West Germany while the Soviet Union occupied East Germany. The 65th Infantry Regiment stayed in Germany for a few months to assist the military government in command of West Germany. While in Germany, soldier Octavio Negrón recalls going to see movies about cowboys and listening to the radio, where he heard both American and traditional German music.

On October 27, 1945, the 65th sailed from France back home to Puerto Rico. Excited crowds received them with cheers and festivities in the streets of San Juan on November 9, 1945. Gonzalo Villanueva, with his feet healed, was glad to be back home. The crowds greeted them like heroes with hundreds of people flooding the streets. Parades and bands played to welcome them home. "We arrived at Puerto Rico and they were waiting for us with fanfare and great enthusiasm, It was a tremendous welcoming," recalled Lieutenant Colonel Tomás Guffain.

Despite being mostly assigned to noncombat missions due to the segregation of the US Army at the time, the 65th Infantry had proven a brave and formidable fighting force. Many of its men returned as decorated soldiers. The 65th Infantry Regiment was awarded some of the highest awards for bravery, including a Distinguished Service Cross and two Silver Stars, as well as several Bronze Stars and Purple Hearts. It would be another five years before the start of the Korean War, but the 65th Infantry found ways to distinguish themselves even between wars.

CHAPTER 2
Operation PORTREX

It is hereby declared to be the policy of the President that there shall be equality of treatment and opportunity for all persons in the armed services without regard to race, color, religion or national origin.

—Executive Order 9981, Desegregation of the Armed Forces, July 26, 1948

A small island sits only 8 miles (13 km) off the coast of Puerto Rico. About 21 miles (34 km) long and 4 miles (6 km) wide, it shimmers with turquoise-blue water and powder-white beaches. Palm trees and other tropical trees and plants cover the island and sway in the warm Caribbean breeze. Wild horses roam and feast off mango and other fruit trees. Called Vieques, it sits just off the east coast of Puerto Rico.

In the 1940s, large, lush, green sugar plantations covered most of the land on this small island and most of its inhabitants were poor laborers who lived and worked on the plantations but owned no land. In 1941 the US government bought land on the east and west end of the island. Just two landowners, the Benitez family and the company Eastern Sugar

Associates, owned most of the land. Although the workers had built houses for themselves and their families on the plantations, they had no legal land titles or deeds, so when the United States purchased the land, it evicted them and forced them to find new homes.

After World War II, the US military staged large training tests, called exercises or maneuvers, on the land. One of the largest military exercises ever performed was on Vieques from February 25 to March 12, 1950. The exercise, code named Operation PORTREX (Puerto Rico Exercise), cast many thousands of soldiers, sailors, pilots, and marines as well as several hundred planes to act in this practice battle on Vieques. The battle squared an army of Liberators against an opposing force called the Aggressors.

The 65th were cast as the Aggressor soldiers and would be led by Brigadier General Edwin L. Sibert. Serving under him were Colonel William W. Harris, who had been appointed as the commander of the 65th Infantry Regiment in July 1949, and Lieutenant Colonel George Childs. The Aggressors were to pretend they had captured Vieques and defend it against the Liberators, who would launch a counterinvasion. The Liberators were from other units in the US military. Their goal was to force the Aggressors off the island.

The script for the exercise instructed the Aggressors to stay in the center of the island and create fences and obstacles to impede the Liberators as they invaded from the east. This type of maneuver allowed both sides to establish defensive positions while being protected by scheduled aerial bombardment. And since it was an exercise, the raining down of bombs, shells, and missiles would be fake. All the men would use inflatable rubber tanks and guns as well as artillery sound and flash simulators to make the exercise seem more realistic. Military officers, called umpires, evaluated the maneuvers, and determined the "casualties" and "damage" to military vehicles and tanks.

But it wasn't meant to be a fair fight. The Liberators outnumbered the Aggressors four to one. And the 65th Infantry Regiment was pitted

> "It was clearly evident . . . that Aggressor was expected and scheduled to lose the battle."

against two of the most decorated divisions from World War II, the 3rd Infantry Division and the 82nd Airborne Division. As Harris saw right away, "It was clearly evident . . . that Aggressor was expected and scheduled to lose the battle."

The Pentagon brass referred to the 65th Infantry Regiment disparagingly as a "rum and Coca-Cola outfit," and when he was first assigned to lead the regiment, Harris thought his career was over.

But the ambitious forty-two-year-old US Military Academy graduate quickly found the 65th to be a well-functioning unit of exceptional soldiers. He earned their favor by reversing the military's ban, under penalty of court-martial, on speaking Spanish. This decision "had an immediate and effective impact on the men . . . the response to this revocation amazed [Harris]."

Facing overwhelming odds, the commanders of the Aggressors knew they had to play it smart. They created a strategy that they thought would easily push the Liberators off the island.

Over the next couple of months, the 65th Infantry arranged and designed their defensive positions, studied their land and terrain, created backup plans, built command posts that protected them from the Liberators' gunfire, and constructed observation posts in the hills to watch the Liberators as they attacked the island.

The men mapped out the best places around the island where they expected the Liberators to land. In the drop zones that paratroopers might land in from the air, the 65th set up nonlethal booby traps and barbed wire. The soft, sandy beaches with the gentlest slopes were where the navy forces would most likely land. From those spots, the 65th determined the best paths and routes into the island that the Liberators might take. Tall coconut trees lined the edge of the beaches. The 65th cut down many of the trees, leaving behind 7-foot (2 m) stumps that they could cover with barbed wire. To further slow the Liberators, the

Aggressors created tank traps by digging large holes in the sand and camouflaging them.

After they built their defenses, they dug and constructed their underground command posts. Here they had radios, desks, and chairs. Metal sheets covered with a few inches of dirt and held up by supporting posts hid the command posts from the invaders' view. The men ran wiring into the command posts to install electricity and the telephones.

After they completed the construction, the troops created and practiced different types of communication, from phones and radios to signal flags, sun mirrors, and smoke signals. The men were as prepared as they could be for the beginning of the exercise.

Before the exercises began, Sibert created some unusual plans. He persuaded Waller Booth, a former Office of Strategic Services officer living in San Juan, to come on active duty and organize an undercover counterespionage network of about sixty agents among the native residents of Vieques who lived in the center of the island.

About a mile (1.6 km) inland in a heavily wooded area, Booth created a training camp for the agents. They had uniforms that looked like Liberators' uniforms. The agents were instructed to mix and socialize with the Liberators, acquiring information to bring back to Booth. This created, as Sibert later said, "a steady flow of intelligence to our headquarters."

The Liberators also tried sneaky moves in the days leading up to the exercise. They sent two undercover agents posing as tourists from San Juan. But before the Liberators' agents could observe the Aggressors' defenses or make their way into the exercise area, the agents trained by Booth spotted and stopped the agents. A couple of nights before the exercise began, the Liberators sent about one hundred frogmen, military men with underwater tactical training, to the beaches to investigate and explore. But because of the camouflage and obstacles the Aggressors had built on the shore, they could not see the hidden machine guns.

On March 8 at dawn, the thunderous booms of bombs woke Harris.

Soon he received a call from his 1st Battalion commander, Colonel Howard St. Clair, informing him that the Liberators' assault boats were just offshore. The Liberators were approaching the island just where the Aggressors had predicted they would.

Once the Liberators reached the beach, their paratroopers floated down into the expected drop zones. A thousand paratroopers and their white parachutes dotted the powder-blue sky.

The Caribbean trade winds proved difficult for the paratroopers to navigate. As a *New York Times* article described at the time, "Umpires judged that the battalion's casualties, had this 'war' been real instead of mimic, might have reached 50 per cent or more, and other observers believed the whole battalion would have been wiped out." The landing forces could not aid the paratroopers due to the obstacles on the beaches, and the Aggressors captured as many of them as they could. "The invaders also suffered heavily on the beaches, which were protected by probably the heaviest field fortifications ever constructed for a maneuver," the *New York Times* said.

Lieutenant Colonel Romeo "Rick" H. Bucknell Jr. later said, "We were supposed to jump, take the island, and run off the winners. But it so happened that they were . . . so well trained, so well dug in, they made us look bad."

Several hours later, St. Clair called Harris again to tell him that the Liberators had been held up by not just the beach defenses but also their own bombing. "Instead of knocking holes in our defenses," he told Harris, "the bombings had made [the beaches] completely impassable."

The Liberators tried to get through the obstacles that the Aggressors built to slow them. Much to their surprise, the soldiers of the 65th Infantry Regiment were so well trained and prepared that

The soldiers of the 65th Infantry Regiment were so well trained and prepared that they kept the Liberators from getting past the Vieques beaches.

Paratroopers descend upon Vieques. The Aggressors' traps surprised them and even injured some, though not very seriously.

they kept the Liberators from getting past the Vieques beaches. "There is not much doubt in actual war casualties would have been heavy . . . the first day's land fighting of Portrex went to the defenders of Vieques."

This was the opposite of how the exercise was supposed to go. The senior Aggressor umpire called an administrative halt to the training so Harris's troops could clear paths through the obstacles and allow the assaulting troops to disembark onshore, making it possible to continue the practice exercises on land. The 65th pulled the obstacles apart using their tanks, wire cutters, and saws. They hooked the tanks up to the large masses of tangled barbed wire and wreckage to pull it apart. They cleared several lanes. By late afternoon the exercise had restarted, this time with the Liberators able to advance farther into the island and fight in coordinated "combat" with the Aggressor troops.

Sibert concocted another sneaky scheme. On the morning of March 10, a stealth agent, dressed in plain clothes as a worker, journeyed to the Liberators' command post. There, the Liberator commander, Major General P. W. Clarkson, was discussing the combat situation with the commander of all invasion forces, Lieutenant General John R. Hodges, and the commander of the amphibious forces, Rear Admiral Harold D. U. Baker. The agent politely saluted Clarkson and handed him a briefcase.

"Here's something for you," he said, as if it was a gift to show appreciation, and then quickly disappeared.

Clarkson opened the briefcase. To his surprise, he found a note saying, "This is a booby trap—you are now dead." The fake bomb in the case "killed" everyone within 100 yards (91 m). But, since this was just an exercise, about an hour later the umpires restored the men to life, allowing them to continue in their roles as the Liberator leaders.

As the fighting continued, the Aggressors gave it their all. By the middle of the day on March 10, Harris could see they were tiring and reaching the end of their endurance. But he had one last trick up his sleeve. During training, he had asked his supply officer, Major Agustín Ramírez, to organize a provisional battalion of about 550 truck drivers, cooks, and other personnel. He ordered that this battalion be trained as a reserve unit.

When the Aggressors had reached their last defensive position before the Liberators could drive them off the island, Harris reached out to Ramírez to use the provisional battalion. Ramírez planned to have the artillery send a heavy barrage as a column of companies from the provisional battalion moved to hit the Liberators' left flank. They would enact the strategy first thing in the morning on March 11.

That night was quiet. The bangs and roars of bombs accompanied the light of daybreak. The final battle began. Harris was ready to give the green light to activate the provisional battalion. But before he could, the umpires ended the exercise and declared the Aggressors victorious.

The 65th had won. There wasn't a prize, but they earned major bragging rights for rebuffing the Liberators and keeping them off the island. Operation PORTREX showed that the Puerto Rican–born soldiers of the 65th Infantry Regiment were well trained and could be just as successful in a combat role as the soldiers from some of the most elite regiments in the US military.

One of the main purposes of Operation PORTREX was to train soldiers, sailors, aviators, and marines to work together. With this goal, Operation PORTREX was a success, even though it didn't go according to plan. The *New York Times* said, "Probably the greatest benefit of the maneuvers was the 'cross education' of the services. . . . Officers of the Air Force, some of them with stars on their shoulders, who had never before worked with the Navy, came to have an understanding of naval problems and vice versa. PORTREX was a training in teamwork which will someday pay off."

Liberator forces storm the beach of Vieques during Operation PORTREX.

Several months later, the Liberators and the Aggressors of Operation PORTREX would fight together in the Korean War.

Meanwhile, back on the mainland of the United States, the fight for civil rights continued. Under political pressure, President Harry Truman signed an executive order in July 1948 to desegregate the military. Although Truman made racist statements and privately supported segregation in his youth, he needed Black voters to win reelection in 1948, and signing the executive order was a strategic move to earn their votes. Despite the executive order, various sects of the military resisted and delayed the integration. Desegregation was only partially complete by the time North Korean forces crossed the border into South Korea in late June 1950. The 65th Infantry Regiment still primarily hailed from Puerto Rico.

CHAPTER 3
Prelude to War

After taking manpower and equipment shortfalls into account, Harris believed the [PORTREX] exercises helped the 65th Infantry to reach a level of combat effectiveness superior to most U.S. Army infantry regiments when the Korean War broke out.

—Colonel Gilberto Villahermosa

T he smoke lifted. The sky cleared. The birds returned to the beaches of Vieques, and the coqui sang. The soldiers of the 65th Infantry Regiment were still energized from the Vieques maneuver when they heard the US had agreed to support South Korea against the invading forces from the north.

The Korean peninsula juts into the Pacific Ocean on the northeast border of China, surrounded on the east by the Sea of Japan and on the west by the Yellow Sea. The peninsula had become a protectorate of Japan after the Russo-Japanese War (1904–1905) and was formally annexed by the Japanese Empire from 1910 until the end of World War II.

After the Soviet Union declared war on Japan and the United States dropped two atomic bombs on the Japanese cities of Hiroshima and Nagasaki, killing ultimately hundreds of thousands of people—mostly civilians—Japan surrendered to the Allied forces. Both the US and the Soviet Union claimed the Korean peninsula, intending to occupy the territory until Korea could become an independent country. By August 1945, the two sides agreed to split Korea into two halves based upon an arbitrary line: the 38th parallel north. The Soviet Union helped North Korea set up a government with its own strong military, and the United States military occupied South Korea and squashed any resistance to their rule. Each region had its own government supported by each superpower, and each government considered itself the rightful governing body of the whole Korean peninsula. The US and the Soviet Union were supposed to work together to help Korea transition into a unified, independent nation, but they were also enemies in the ongoing Cold War. Negotiations failed, and the two sides of the split Korea became hostile to each other. Once the leader of North Korea, Kim Il-sung, received support from Soviet leader Joseph Stalin, he launched the attack into South Korea. Stalin assumed that the United States would get involved in the conflict, but did not expect the force of its response.

On June 25, 1950, the North Korean People's Army (NKPA) invaded South Korea with the financial and political support of the Soviet Union and China. The United Nations (UN) condemned the attack and called for international support of South Korea. After a vote at which the Soviet Union was not present, the UN authorized the creation of the United Nations Command (UNC), a military force composed of the militaries of several member countries of the UN. As one of the largest UN members, the United States would lead the UNC forces and provide most of the military personnel and equipment. Truman appointed General Douglas MacArthur as the commander of the UNC.

The NKPA quickly advanced their position, moving farther and farther into South Korea. The United States had some occupying forces to support the South Korean Army, but the NKPA moved aggressively and captured the South Korean capital of Seoul by June 28, 1950.

On September 15, 1950, the branches of the US military led a combined assault on the west coast of Korea near Incheon, attacking by land, sea, and air. They cut off North Korean supply lines and forced the NKPA north. Soon after, the US military recaptured Seoul for South Korea. But MacArthur decided to push north into North Korea. This led to a successful campaign pushing north, but it also caused one of the most disastrous turns in the war.

When news came that the United States was joining the UNC to support South Korea, the 65th Regiment received their orders from the Department of Defense. The regiment was to clean up the Vieques

Refugees sometimes crossed the 38th parallel, and soldiers would check them for contraband. The 38th parallel continues to divide North and South Korea. Around the border is a demilitarized zone designed to maintain a buffer between the two sides.

The Battle of Incheon was a huge military assault that resulted in victory for the United Nations forces. Pictured here are UN forces unloading during the invasion.

battlefield. Their principal mission was to repaint and repair government buildings, mow lawns, and chase away any stray dogs or wandering civilians who crossed onto the military grounds. "We were humiliated," Harris noted later in his memoir, "by being told that the regiment was to be relegated to the level of a mere caretaking establishment."

To add insult to injury, the Pentagon had also reduced the unit's size for fiscal reasons. This disappointed the soldiers but did not deter them. They began their new assignments that spring.

But this custodial role would not last long. Sibert called Harris to tell him they had to cancel the fishing trip they had planned for Puerto Rico and the US Virgin Islands. "You and I are wanted on a three-way teleconference with Panama and the Pentagon," Sibert said somberly in his native southern accent. Harris wondered what this could mean as he entered the telecom room.

The Structure of the Army

The US Army is organized by a hierarchy of military units. An officer commands each unit.

- **Team:** Four soldiers, including one noncommissioned officer (NCO)
- **Squad:** Two teams and up to ten soldiers, commanded by a staff sergeant
- **Platoon:** Two to three squads, totaling up to thirty-six soldiers, commanded by a lieutenant
- **Company:** Three to four platoons and up to two hundred soldiers, commanded by a captain
- **Battalion:** Four to six companies, totaling up to one thousand soldiers, commanded by a lieutenant colonel
- **Brigade:** Two to three battalions, totaling up to three thousand soldiers, commanded by a colonel and sometimes called a regiment
- **Division:** Three to four brigades, totaling up to fifteen thousand soldiers, commanded by a major general
- **Corps:** Two to five divisions, totaling up to forty-five thousand soldiers, commanded by a lieutenant general
- **Field army:** Four or more divisions, totaling about ninety thousand soldiers, commanded by a general

There was no video conferencing at the time. Instead, in the room stood a big white movie theater screen on which outgoing and incoming messages appeared in text. Seated next to the screen was the typist who operated the teleconference equipment. Sibert walked into the room right before the teleconference began. Anxiously waiting for the text messages to appear on the screen, Sibert in a foreshadowing moment turned to Harris. "You know," he said thoughtfully, "I have been thinking about a reason for this conference, and the only logical conclusion that I can reach is that the 65th is headed for Korea."

They soon had their answer. The names of the people on the conference appeared on the screen. Then their orders appeared:

YOU ARE DIRECTED TO PREPARE THE 65TH INFANTRY REGIMENT FOR AN OVERSEAS ASSIGNMENT. DESTINATION: UNKNOWN (SECRET). . . . THE PLAN IS FOR THE 65TH INFANTRY TO MOVE TO AN UNKNOWN DESTINATION OVERSEAS, THERE TO JOIN UP WITH THE 3RD UNITED STATES INFANTRY DIVISION AND GO THROUGH A CYCLE OF BASIC TRAINING BEFORE ONWARD MOVEMENT TO YOUR FINAL DESTINATION (SECRET). . . . YOU WILL BE PREPARED TO SAIL WITHIN TEN DAYS' TIME. . . . THE 3RD BATTALION, 33RD INFANTRY IN PANAMA IS HEREBY DETACHED FROM THAT ORGANIZATION AND ASSIGNED TO THE 65TH UNITED STATES INFANTRY REGIMENT (SECRET).

Harris was pleased to have the support and assistance of the 33rd Infantry Regiment. But he worried that ten days would not be enough for the 65th and the 33rd Regiments to train together. Further, the Pentagon informed Sibert and Harris that the men would be traveling outloaded, meaning they would travel on separate ships than the ones that would carry their equipment. Harris preferred the ship carrying the men to be combat-loaded, or have the men travel with their heavy equipment. If the ships became separated on the journey and the men arrived in Korea to a firefight, they would not have their battle equipment. Once the instructions from the Pentagon ended, Harris fired off a series of questions.

QUESTION: REQUEST 65TH INFANTRY BE ALLOWED TO COMBAT-LOAD (SECRET).

On the other end was silence. Were they discussing it? Were they trying to accommodate the request? Ten minutes went by before the response: "Negative."

Harris shook his head, but he pushed on with his other question.

QUESTION: REQUEST AUTHORIZATION TO RECRUIT PERSONNEL WITH AT LEAST SIX MONTHS PS [PREVIOUS SERVICE] TO BRING REGIMENT TO FULL STRENGTH PLUS 10 PERCENT OVERSTRENGTH. END OF QUESTION (SECRET).

Silence again. Then the response came: "Approved."

Harris breathed a sigh of relief. The teleconference ended. It was time to execute their orders. The 65th Infantry Regiment was heading overseas.

The affirmative answer to Harris's second question meant that the 65th was approved to have almost four thousand troops. At the time, the regiment only had ninety-two officers and 1,895 enlisted soldiers. Harris moved quickly to increase enlistment. Radio broadcasters publicized the open recruitment into the 65th Infantry throughout Puerto Rico.

By the next morning, droves of men reported to the fort. The island had always been famous for its amazing patriotism, sporting some of the highest volunteer enlistment numbers of any state or territory in the US. In August 1950 that patriotism was on full display. Hundreds lined up down the streets and around the corners. But the 65th Infantry could not accept all of them. So, Sibert created a soldier replacement center at Camp Tortuguero, a military station in Vega Baja, Puerto Rico. There, experienced soldiers trained new recruits who could replace soldiers who either ended their tour of duty or were injured or killed.

Many of the Puerto Rican men volunteered because of the allure of the army. Former soldier Nicolas Santiago-Rosario said, "As a youth, I watched the soldiers of the 65th Infantry Regiment [conduct] maneuvers in the outskirts of my hometown in Puerto Rico. The pomp and pageantry, crisp uniforms, snappy salutes, the glitter of brass, spit-polished boots, precision drills, the firing of weapons, and the prospects of travel were allures that I could not resist. I wished then that someday I would become a soldier to serve my country."

The enlistment of the men happened quickly since they were to set sail within ten days of receiving the order to mobilize. Within that short time, the 65th Infantry Regiment enlisted over eighteen hundred new recruits. The regiment then consisted of three battalions of about one thousand soldiers each. Once again, Puerto Rico was ready to go to war for the US's allies.

In late August, the 65th Infantry Regiment prepared to embark on their second overseas mission ever. It took twelve hours for the 65th to board the USNS *Marine Lynx* and load their supplies onto the ship.

Some of the men from the 65th Infantry Regiment before deployment to Korea.

The soldiers carried their barrack bags filled with essentials as well as small keepsakes that would remind them of their beloved island. Their uniforms included long-sleeved, button-up shirts; slacks; and matching hats. Many of them packed guitars and fiddles to play in their off time. At three in the morning on August 23, the 3,880 soldiers set sail for an unknown destination. "We didn't know where we were going," Manuel Rivera-Santiago remembered. Many of the men stared across the ocean as they sailed away from the island, watching the shadows of the mountains and El Morro disappear from the dark horizon.

The boat was jam-packed with soldiers and their belongings for the long trip. Beds were limited on the ship, so the men slept in shifts, sharing bunks. According to retired soldier Benjamin Pagan Ayala, "The chow line [for meals in the cafeteria] never stopped, you had so many soldiers. There were soldiers having breakfast at two or three in the afternoon. It was a real mess." In their off time, usually in the evening, they would watch movies, attend church services, and create live shows to keep one another entertained.

When the men were not sleeping or eating, they trained. The soldiers practiced cleaning, assembling, and caring for weapons. They executed marksmanship exercises, conducted bayonet training, and practiced organizing and training the mortar company.

They also prepared for worst-case scenarios. They staged battlefield casualties and practiced carrying injured soldiers to safety. They learned to create arm and leg splints from crates and pitched makeshift first aid tents for the wounded.

The commanders also trained the men not to trust anyone. They updated the men regularly on the ambush-style attacks the North Koreans had been using against US forces in Korea. "Willy-nilly, our troops would march down the road and pay little or no attention to the seemingly harmless, baggy-drawered men, women, and children until suddenly some of them whipped out burp guns, pistols, and hand grenades and dry-gulched our soldiers," Harris said.

They restarted their weekly staff meetings with the noncommissioned officers, enlisted soldiers who usually did not come from a military school. These meetings helped maintain open communication between the military leaders (the continental officers, including the three battalion commanders) and the senior NCOs (the sergeants and corporals). Many of the NCOs and continental officers were bilingual, and some were veterans of World War II. During one of these meetings, they officially adopted the battle name Borinqueneers for the 65th Infantry Regiment. Borinqueneer is a portmanteau, a combination of two words. The first word, Borinquen, is Taíno for Puerto Rico. Many of the men of the 65th Infantry were of Taíno descent. The second word, *buccaneer*, is the name for the Spanish sea pirates who sailed the Caribbean in the 1600s. Combined, Borinqueneer reflected both the men's ancestry and their determination in battle.

The long voyage led them through the Panama Canal. There, the 33rd Infantry Regiment joined them. On August 30, some of the men moved to another boat, the USNS *Sergeant Howard E. Woodford*, to help ease crowding. They shipped off again the next day.

They continued their journey across the Pacific Ocean to Japan. Once they arrived in Sasebo,

Bitter Extremes

The sweltering heat of South Korea during the summer can be unbearable with temperatures soaring above 100°F (38°C). The frigid cold of North Korea in the mountains drops to a painful 40°F (4°C) during the winter. In 1950 winter arrived early in mid-November. The steep and jagged Taebaek Mountains stretch along the east coast of Korea. Some sharp peaks reach 5,000 feet (1,524 m) high. The 65th Infantry Regiment fought in both scorching hot and bitter cold weather in Korea.

Lieutenant Dan H. Bonner (*right*) assesses the additional troops that were attached to the 65th Infantry Regiment en route to Korea. The soldiers were from all over the continental US and other US-held territories.

Japan, on September 15, Harris sent Childs onshore to receive their next set of orders. Childs was onshore for two hours before returning to the captain's boat to report to Harris. They had guessed right: they were headed to Korea.

Childs told Harris that the battalion from Panama had been delayed and would not arrive for at least another week. And that wasn't the only bad news. The 65th Infantry's equipment ship had been delayed as well, by about four days. And they still didn't know where they would be sent after arriving in Korea.

Harris shook his head. His fears had come true. They would be arriving in Korea soon without most of their equipment and many of their personnel. They would need to make do.

On September 23, not long after they left Sasebo, the USNS *Marine Lynx* and the USNS *Sergeant Howard E. Woodford* pulled into the harbor at Pusan, Korea. Small adobe huts dotted the landscape. The little

straw-covered houses with clay chimneys sat in the villages on dirt roads that the Korean people rode their bikes down, peddling hard with their thin, rubber moccasins. Farmers continued their work in rice paddies. Hundreds of refugees who had fled from NKPA forces were wandering the dusty streets in and around Pusan.

Once in Pusan, Harris eagerly awaited his orders about where the Borinqueneers were going and who they would be fighting. He had learned on the journey over that the 65th Infantry Regiment was assigned

Even as the 65th Infantry Regiment arrived in Pusan, the city was bustling. Soldiers, refugees, and working citizens crowded the streets, walking past still-burning buildings from recent attacks.

to the 8th United States Army, the commanding formation and field army made up of all US forces stationed in South Korea. That meant Harris answered to Lieutenant General Walton Walker, the commander of the 8th Army.

Harris met with Walker for orders. Walker pointed out his window and said, "Do you see those trains?"

Harris nodded.

"Get on them and go that way," Walker said, and pointed northward.

CHAPTER 4
The First Battles

The 65th had an excellent reputation with the Chinese [forces]. They did not like to fight the 65th. They [the 65th] were too mean. I was very glad the Puerto Ricans were on my side. I would not want them to come after me with abandon.

—Colonel Willis Cronkhite Jr.

North Korea and South Korea had well-developed rail lines that both sides used during the Korean War to transport troops and supplies. Because many roads were in poor condition for military use, rail was the primary method of transport during the first year of the Korean War. It was a reliable means of transportation. But North Korean forces knew where the rail lines were, and that left them vulnerable to attacks.

The soldiers, following Walker's orders, boarded the trains with their hard hats on and their backpacks strapped on tight. The slow, rickety passenger trains carrying the 2nd Battalion of the 65th Infantry Regiment chugged northward, entering a valley with large, steep hills on both sides. They were the first soldiers of the 65th to head north, and the rest of the Borinqueneers would join them soon. But they had only traveled about 10 miles (16 km) before hearing the rat-a-tat-tat-tat of gunfire blasting from both sides of the train. Windows shattered inward, showering glass over the soldiers. They ducked for cover as the train stopped.

Harris later recalled the suddenness of the attack. "The crash of the splintering glass and the thud of the bullets as they struck the side of the car were all the proof we needed [that we were under attack] as we hit the deck and scurried for cover, flat on the floor, under our seats, and even in the toilets—which were actually worse than the possibility of being hit by a bullet."

After the shock of the unforeseen attack wore off, the 2nd Battalion sprang into action. Some soldiers stayed inside the train cars, shooting out of the broken windows at the enemy. This kept the North Korean aggressors engaged in a fight while other soldiers stealthily sneaked out the back of the train and flanked the enemy. After thirty minutes of intense exchange of fire, the 65th Infantry Regiment drove the enemy back. The train was damaged but still functional. It resumed its journey and carried the battalion farther north to their destination of Samnangjin. The battalion suffered no casualties. One battle down but many more to come.

The 1st Battalion arrived at dusk without incident. In late September the IX Corps attached the reunited 65th Infantry Regiment to the larger 2nd Infantry Division, commanded by Major General Laurence B. Keiser. He had a specific plan for the 65th Regiment: they were to fight the NKPA at Hill 409 and support the rest of the 2nd Infantry Division, which was already fighting there. Finally, they had clear orders. The Borinqueneers were officially being sent into battle.

When the 65th arrived at Hill 409 and relieved the unit that was holding the hill, the scene was hectic. They had orders to stop the enemy from retreating and capture as many enemy soldiers as possible, and units

Trucks carry troops from the 65th Infantry Regiment across the Naktong River, heading north to engage the NKPA and the PVA forces.

were crisscrossing one another in their attempts to track down NKPA units. But the NKPA had separated into small guerrilla units hiding in the hills, making it difficult to track them down.

During daylight hours the 65th searched for and fought the enemy. After several days, they realized that the enemy units were all moving in a clear direction: north. They were retreating! With the arrival of the Borinqueneers, the enemy forces had realized they were suddenly facing a more prepared and better supplied opponent than before.

But even though the 65th had the upper hand, they couldn't let their guard down. They had to somehow protect themselves from surprise attacks while they slept on the battlefield at night. Harris came up with an idea. He explained to the soldiers how when early settlers in the western United States "halted for the night, they pulled their wagons into a tight

> With the arrival of the Borinqueneers, the enemy forces had realized they were suddenly facing a more prepared and better supplied opponent than before.

circle as a barricade." The 65th did the same thing with their vehicles, creating a protective barrier for the soldiers inside. They made sure to set up camp on high ground, too, so that enemy forces couldn't strike inside the circles from above.

The Borinqueneers had barely any time to celebrate their first successful operation before they were sent to fight again. On October 3, they were ordered to support a unit near their location. They approached the enemy from the rear, boxing the North Korean soldiers in so they could not retreat. The enemy quickly surrendered and became prisoners of war (POWs).

As the 65th fought in its first battles, the tank company battalion from Panama finally arrived in Korea, bringing tanks, artillery, and engineers to support the rest of the unit. With their arrival, the unit was fully prepared for combat. Their strength was bolstered not only with the new equipment but also with the increased personnel, many of whom came from US territories all over the world. While it was still a mostly Puerto Rican outfit, Black Americans, US Virgin Islanders, and many others fought together in the mostly Puerto Rican unit.

On October 9 a reconnaissance group found a camp of two thousand NKPA soldiers near Waegwan, South Korea. Using all three battalions, the 65th Regiment boxed in the NKPA forces at the Naktong River. This attack took almost the whole month to execute, and the NKPA put up a tough fight the entire time, using unexpected and upsetting strategies. They separated into guerrilla units that were hard to track down, and they would attack at the darkest point of night when most of the soldiers of the 65th were asleep. At the beginning of each strike, rows of soldiers blew whistles and hurled bloodcurdling screams to scare and confuse their enemies. Initially, this caught the 65th off guard, but they quickly adapted to this strategy and made real-time adjustments as the enemy fought them. The 65th Infantry quickly gained a reputation within the US Army as, according to Harris, "cool, determined, self-reliant, and effective combat soldiers."

By late October, the war seemed to be going well for the US. The UNC forces led by MacArthur had pushed the NKPA nearly as far north as the Yalu River, part of Korea's border with China. The fighting along the Naktong River slowed, and the 65th received new orders to move back toward Pusan. They were also moved out of the 2nd Infantry Division and placed in X Corps, commanded by Major General Edward M. Almond. As they were arriving in Pusan, they heard the news: China had entered the war.

> As they were arriving in Pusan, they heard the news: China had entered the war.

This development caught the US by surprise. On October 19, 1950, an army of Chinese forces, the PVA, crossed the Yalu River into North Korea to support the NKPA. Because China didn't want to officially declare war on the United States, it claimed that the PVA was composed of volunteer forces from China and, therefore, not an official military force. But official or not, it massively increased the strength and numbers of the forces fighting on the side of the NKPA.

The war had changed. UNC forces were no longer able to easily push the NKPA north. Counterattacks from PVA forces halted their progress and might soon turn the tide in favor of North Korea. This new development meant yet another change of plans for the Borinqueneers. From Pusan, the Borinqueneers were ordered to sail to Wonsan, North Korea, and then travel from Wonsan 60 miles (97 km) north to the inland town of Yonghung. There, they were to fight alongside other units in the 8th Army against two PVA armies that were coming south. The 8th Army was already in position, and the Borinqueneers had to get moving to meet up with them. They were to meet with the 1st Calvary Division, but they did not have reliable information about the 1st Calvary's exact location. They only knew they were somewhere west of Yonghung.

They were also not told the exact size of the enemy presence in the region. But Harris knew that two PVA armies comprised six corps, each with three infantry divisions and each division with about ten thousand soldiers. So, they would be facing a force of roughly two hundred thousand PVA soldiers. If they encountered the PVA alone, the Borinqueneers would be outnumbered thirty-three to one.

They would have to plan en route and hope for the best.

Harris flew to the X Corps headquarters in Wonsan while the 65th Infantry Regiment sailed to meet him. One morning, while waiting for the 65th to land in Wonsan, he took a walk and came upon a large radio truck on the side of the road with its two operators and driver sitting under a tree. The truck was equipped with technology capable of sending and receiving radio messages across the entire Korean peninsula. When the radio operators heard who Harris was, they were amazed. They had heard a lot about the 65th Infantry Regiment over the radio and were impressed by its reputation. "They must be some fighters," one man said.

While pleased to hear about his unit's reputation, Harris was intrigued about their radio system. The 65th Infantry Regiment's radios did not have the same capabilities. Harris knew communication capabilities were important to any regiment, and he convinced the operators and driver to come with the 65th to Yonghung. Unbeknownst to all of them, this hidden gem would pay off later.

The 65th's 2.5-ton (2.3 t) trucks traveled in a straight line on the one road from Wonsan to Yonghung from sunrise to sunset. Traveling on an open road in broad daylight was risky. Allied commanders knew that NKPA and PVA forces always lurked on high ground in the hills and mountains, waiting for the Allied forces to approach their positions. But they had no other option. The off-road area in the region between Wonsan and Yonghung was wet, muddy, and full of rice paddy fields. The trucks were too heavy to travel off-road through the paddies without sinking or getting stuck. The rest of the landscape was open and bare of vegetation. The men started their journey from Wonsan at three in the morning, hoping that by traveling at least partially in the dark, enemy forces would be less likely to spot them.

Chinese citizens bid farewell to soldiers in the PVA as they head to Korea.

Radio operators were crucial to ensuring coordination between battles, getting help to troops in trouble, and informing the world outside of the war of the events taking place.

They had almost reached Yonghung when the sun emerged from the horizon, slowly illuminating barren terrain on the road between steep mountains. The 65th Regiment's vehicles approached a deep valley flanked on both sides by the tall, steep, and jagged Taebaek Mountains. The air was quiet and still. Then the soldiers heard a distant whizz. They had no time to react before the incoming mortar fire exploded along the road, sending them flying out of their jeeps and into a ditch. The 65th crawled and scrambled to find cover while the rapid beat of machine-gun fire echoed in the hills and mortar shells threw billows of dirt into the air. A small guerrilla unit of about a dozen enemy soldiers occupied a hill above them. The higher elevation helped the NKPA trap the men under fire.

Suddenly, shots rang out from the trucks' flanks and soldiers began to yell. Emerging from the muck on either side of the road, soldiers leaped from their hiding spots and fired back at the guerrilla unit. Before they left Wonsan, small groups of Borinqueneers went ahead of the trucks and along the vehicles' flanks in case the enemy planned an ambush. The NKPA were caught off guard by the 65th's clever plan. They hadn't been expecting to be ambushed back.

The NKPA were caught off guard by the 65th's clever plan. They hadn't been expecting to be ambushed back.

It took most of the day, but the Borinqueneers finally pushed the enemy into a retreat. Once the road was clear again, they got back into the trucks and continued another three hours before arriving in Yonghung in the late afternoon on November 6. Then they discovered that while they were traveling, Almond had directed the 1st and 3rd Battalions to an area 10 miles (16 km) away from Yonghung,

Meanwhile, the soldiers of the 2nd Battalion drove around the village, looking for a safe place to set up camp for the evening. The village of Yonghung was larger than they expected. About four thousand small huts covered the area. The villagers and farmers milled around as if it were a normal day. On the west end of the village stood a hill. As the men drove up the hill, they found abandoned foxholes and adobe huts. They used the foxholes and huts to set up a perimeter defense. With the cold, precooked canned food, or C rations, in their bellies, they unrolled their army sleeping bags within the foxholes and went to bed under a moonless sky.

The next attack came on November 7 at three thirty in the morning with the familiar hiss of incoming mortars. The men awoke to dirt flying and dust everywhere. The whistles of incoming rifle fire accompanied the mortars. The men quickly shimmied out of their sleeping bags and sprang into action.

The firepower initially came from the west but was quickly joined by shots from all sides. The shadows of enemy soldiers flickered in the darkness—some three thousand men had descended upon them. The Borinqueneers returned machine-gun fire. Typically, they would fire

A patrol from the 3rd Infantry Division, the unit that attached to the 65th Infantry Regiment on the way to Korea, fires at enemy troops that have descended upon a convoy of trucks. Their assistance allows the convoy to continue onward.

mortars back at the enemy. But the regimental mortar company had not been sent with the 2nd Battalion. As the men continued exchanging fire for an hour and a half, Harris began to worry they would run out of ammunition. If the fighting continued at that pace, they would deplete their supply within hours. Thinking fast, he remembered the radio truck and used it to send an urgent priority message to Almond.

"From Harris to Almond," the message read. "Under attack by enemy force estimated at two repeat two regiments. Estimate 2nd Battalion will be out of ammunition by [eight in the morning]. Request emergency airdrop of basic load rifle ammunition comma medical supplies comma and C rations period signed Harris."

They could do nothing but wait. Time crept by as the heavy fighting continued. The sun peaked over the horizon. Just as the light touched the battlefield, Harris heard *whoop, Whoop, WHOOP,* the approach of incoming aircraft.

Seven C-47s, huge military aircraft designed for transporting troops and cargo, flew overhead. They dropped several loads of cargo attached to parachutes that floated toward the struggling soldiers through the smoke and dust of battle. The loads landed nearby on the mountaintop. The men retrieved the ammunition, medical supplies, and C rations that Harris had requested. The men roared and cheered, screaming "Maná del cielo!" (Pennies from heaven!)

As soon as the airdrop came, the enemy retreated, knowing they could no longer wait and starve out the 65th. It was another swift victory for the Borinqueneers. After the fighting ended, Almond visited Harris. They spoke about the firefight that night as well as the 65th. "General Almond said something to [Harris] to the effect that he didn't have much confidence in these colored troops. He said he had a bitter experience with them in Italy and that he didn't trust them."

But Harris explained that they "have fought like real troopers."

The second part of the mission was to move west and assist the 8th Army, who were battling a massive PVA force made up of thousands of

C-47 planes were developed for use during World War II, and the military continued using them for many wars after. They shuttled cargo and paratroopers across war zones, providing supplies and assistance to troops in need.

enemy soldiers. But Harris knew he needed the two diverted battalions for the mission to succeed. Over the next two days, the other two battalions arrived and the 65th continued their mission to extend west.

As they traveled west, they encountered streams of Korean refugees fleeing to the east and south, a clear sign that PVA or NKPA forces were approaching from the same direction.

Knowing they would soon encounter the approaching enemy forces, the commanders of the 65th devised a new, sneaky strategy. During daybreak and dusk, while it was light enough that the enemy could see them, the men loudly dug their foxholes in a high hill and pretended to set up a perimeter defense. They made sure the enemy saw them position themselves. They wanted the enemy to know where they were. Or rather, they wanted the enemy to *think* they knew where they were. But at nightfall, the Borinqueneers quietly crept off the hill and moved to another nearby hill in the dark.

Keeping spirits up was crucial for soldiers to perform well on the battlefield. In between combat assignments, during brief moments of reprieve, soldiers from the 65th found ways to have fun. Here, a group of Borinqueneers play on a schoolyard slide in Yongchon, North Korea.

When the enemy attacked the empty hill where they thought the 65th would be, the Borinqueneers suddenly attacked from behind, startling and confusing the enemy. They quickly overpowered the opposing forces and sent them into retreat. The success of this new strategy impressed Harris, and he used it again several times throughout the war.

In mid-November, Major General Robert Soule, the 3rd Infantry Division commander, met with Harris at his command post in Yonghung. He told Harris that the 65th would again be moved, this time to join with the 3rd Infantry Division. Of all their assignments so far, this one worried Harris the most. The 3rd Infantry Division was the group the

Borinqueneers had practiced with in Operation PORTREX. The 65th Infantry had become famous for upsetting the plans of the 3rd Infantry and humiliating them on the beaches of Vieques. How would the 3rd Infantry receive the 65th?

To his surprise, the 3rd Infantry welcomed the 65th. If the soldiers had held grudges from the victory of the 65th on Vieques, they had let them go as rumors of the Borinqueneers' bravery and accomplishments spread through the 8th Army. But their time with the 3rd Division wouldn't be easy. Winter winds were coming down from the Siberian plains, and the cold Korean winter was setting in.

CHAPTER 5
Losing Ground

Happiness is being ignorant of what the future holds; happiness is walking into the Lions' Den, thinking that the lions are not home; happiness, in this case, was the feeling of false security.

—Brigadier General W. W. Harris (Ret.)

It had been cool when the 65th landed in Korea, but as they moved farther north, they encountered even harsher, more frigid conditions. Winter arrived early that year, and by November they were met with snow and temperatures reaching below zero.

The bone-chilling northern winds from over the Yalu River made the conditions even worse. This was very different from the tropical weather they knew in Puerto Rico. Many of the soldiers came down with pneumonia. Their toes and fingers grew numb with frostbite.

One of the greatest challenges for the 65th Infantry Regiment that winter was the lack of warm clothes. Many of the soldiers had only summer clothes. They did not begin receiving their winter uniforms until late November, and some didn't receive them until early December.

During the winter in Korea, many forms of vehicular transportation became unreliable, and so soldiers would carry supplies to troops on the field.

Soldiers from the 7th Infantry hike up the steep hills that make up much of the North Korean landscape. While climbing up uneven terrain is already difficult, soldiers also had to lug around their uniforms, equipment, and packs, which altogether typically weighed between 80 and 100 pounds (36 and 45 kg).

Even as they slowly started to receive shipments of cold-weather shoes, there weren't enough for all the soldiers. And some days, even the military-issued clothing couldn't keep the cold out. As winter set in, they layered the new clothes on top of their old clothes. "We had so many layers. . . . Three layers of gloves. Four layers of clothing," retired soldier Celestino Cordova later remembered. Many soldiers wore long-sleeved woolen underwear, several layers of wool shirts and trousers, cotton jackets and one or two sweaters, air-insulated overshoes, fur-collared overcoats, mufflers, and pile caps with built-in earmuffs.

"The most we could do was waddle like Christmas-fed ducks," Harris later said. To keep warm, they kept jumping and running back and forth.

Orders from the division commanders directed the troops to keep themselves as warm and comfortable as possible during the winter months, and the Borinqueneers were quick to take the cue. Resourceful and inventive, they created makeshift heating devices out of their military equipment, including several gadgets that used blowtorches and tent stoves. Some soldiers wrapped towels around their heads to create warm hats and protect their ears from frostbite.

The severe conditions only amplified the brutality of the fighting. They fought along the Yonghung-Hadongsan axis, which covered about 900 square miles (2,331 sq. km). During one battle in late November, the enemy besieged and outnumbered the 65th near Kowan. The enemy attacked at the darkest point of night, engaging in heavy fighting for four hours. Twelve soldiers of the 65th were wounded, five of them seriously injured. Calls of "Médico!" echoed in the night. Each time, Sergeant Luis Marrero, a part of the 65th Medical Company, moved quickly among the soldiers to find the wounded and administer first aid. Despite the freezing weather, the shortage of medical supplies, and the heavy fire from the enemy, he patched up his fellow soldiers and carried them to safety. At one point, he grabbed an automatic rifle; jumped on top of a nearby parapet, or protected area; and fired heavily into the opposing forces, causing them to stop attacking briefly.

Meanwhile, the UNC leadership had noticed a gradual buildup of enemy forces. Trying to prepare for whatever this buildup could mean, the X Corps leaders developed several different strategies for various situations and operations. These orders were sent in rapid succession, often before the lower-ranking divisions had time to react to the previous order.

The early successes of the Borinqueneers in the field had kept their spirits high. But during the first few days of December, they began to receive several confusing and contradicting movement orders. In the afternoon of November 30, they were ordered to proceed west 30 miles (48 km) from Yonghung to Songha-dong. On December 1, the leadership of the 65th began planning and preparing the positioning of the troops. As the soldiers were about to head to the village, they received a second order canceling the first and instead directing them north toward the city of Hamhung in North Korea. They rested a few hours as the officers regrouped to change their plans and then proceeded north. But before the entire unit could even leave Yonghung, they received yet another order, this time to proceed south to Wonsan.

The soldiers did not know what to think. Why were the orders changing so rapidly? Was there confusion even at the highest levels of UNC leadership? Or was the enemy overpowering their forces that quickly? Did this mean their forces were being pushed back? The possibilities worried some of the soldiers. Whatever the case, the Borinqueneers turned their columns around and proceeded south. But when the 1st Battalion reached Wonsan, they received a fourth order reversing their direction again to Hamhung. Before midnight on December 5, the entire unit arrived in Hamhung.

> Why were the orders changing so rapidly? . . . Was the enemy overpowering their forces that quickly?

This time, they were to travel north to Hamhung to protect the withdrawal of the 1st Marine Division, which was surrounded by the enemy in the village of Hagaru-ri near the Chosin Reservoir. X Corps had underestimated the size of the enemy, and the 1st Marine Division was trapped. Confused by yet another sudden change but ready to obey their orders, the Borinqueneers quickly turned around and reached Hamhung on December 4, 1950.

To bolster the 65th's strength and provide support, the 3rd Infantry lent them two additional battalions. Harris planned to organize the two units like those in Operation PORTREX. They would create a line for the 1st Marine Division to retreat behind and then protect them while they retreated. The plan required a route be kept cleared between Hagaru-ri to the port in Hungnam, a district of Hamhung, so army and marine units could retreat while PVA forces were advancing south.

Some of the soldiers were stationed on a mountain ridge along the road just south of Majon-dong. The ridge was high enough that they could watch and protect several miles of the evacuation route. It was a

A rifle crew from the 3rd Battalion of the 65th Infantry Regiment readies their gun to defend an outpost.

prime strategic location, so the enemy would try to take it. The soldiers would have to be wary not only of enemy forces along the road but also of those attempting to usurp their position.

In the early hours of December 7, PVA forces attacked. From the top of the ridge, the Borinqueneers fired at the shadowy figures as they attacked from behind them. Wave after wave attacked them all night long. After the marines passed through the evacuation route, the Borinqueneers joined them and followed them to Hamhung. After them came the rear guard: the 1st Platoon, led by Nieves.

When the PVA attacked the retreating troops from the rear, Nieves ordered his platoon to continue retreating behind the column while he moved, alone, to the top of a nearby hill. With his automatic rifle, he continuously rained down bullets on the enemy, sending dust and dirt flying everywhere. The attack and volume of fire was so fierce that he stopped the enemy's forward movement. Nieves single-handedly killed eighteen enemy soldiers and sent the rest running for the hills. Later, Nieves earned the Silver Star for his actions.

The Borinqueneers successfully defended the 1st Marine Division's retreat, but they soon realized this was only part of a much larger withdrawal of UNC troops. As the retreat continued into mid-December, news came that the enemy buildup had accelerated. Chinese and North Korean forces were gathering and converging on Hungnam. The UNC's worst fears were coming true: they were losing ground in the war.

They had to accelerate their plans in response to protect their troops and evacuate the Korean refugees that had fled to Hungnam. They ordered troops to board ships, division by division, and sail south to Pusan. Meanwhile, the 65th and the 3rd Infantry Divisions would hold the main line of resistance, providing enough cover for everyone to make it safely out of Hungnam. The 1st Marine Division left first. Next the supplies, ammunition, and equipment, as well as tens of thousands of North Korean refugees were evacuated. Between December 18 to 21, the 7th Infantry Division boarded a ship for Pusan. With each withdrawal, the enemy continued to push the Borinqueneers and the 3rd Infantry Division.

The night of December 22 was cold, with snow covering the ground and stars glittering like shards of ice. The Borinqueneers were stationed on a snowy hill just outside Hungnam, still protecting the harbor. As they had for the past several days, at the darkest point in the night, PVA forces struck against the Borinqueneers. But this night was different: the enemy soldiers were much more numerous than expected. About two thousand PVA soldiers emerged from the dark and attacked the battalion on the hill.

Crystals of ice and snow flew into the air. The flashes and smoke of gunfire lit the night. The enemy focused their mortars and rifle fire on

The Taebaek Mountains run north to south along the eastern edge of the Korean peninsula. The mountains are steep, heavily forested, and up to 6,500 feet (2 km) high.

the machine gun of Corporal Antonio Santos and his assistant Corporal Gilberto Calderon. A large piece of the mortar flew and hit their machine gun, breaking it.

The two soldiers worked quickly to repair the machine gun. Explosions and rumbles echoed from all directions around them. Ice flew in their eyes and their fingers trembled, nearly frozen. Hearts pounding and under heavy fire, they finally repaired the gun and started shooting back. The enemy scrambled to withdraw, and when the smoke cleared, over half the enemy forces were wounded or dead.

This bloody battle was one of their last at Hungnam. With the other troops withdrawn, it was time for the 3rd Division to begin loading onto boats. The main line of resistance fell back to the perimeter of the harbor.

They were exhausted from several days of fighting. No longer smiling, yet still determined, they finally would board ships in their dirty and tattered uniforms. On the afternoon of December 24, the 65th began loading onto four ships: the USS *Freeman*, the USS *Henrico*, the SS *Hunter Victory*, and the SS *Carleton Victory*. The soldiers of the 65th were some of the last to leave Hungnam. They were hurried and squeezed tightly onto the final boats. Finally, they could rest and relax. Once they left, the military would destroy the port so the enemy could not use the equipment and facilities against them.

The heroic and lifesaving acts of the Borinqueneers earned them great praise at home and within the military.

Years later, retired soldier Rivera-Santiago remembered that Christmas Eve:

> We finally left. Everybody leaving, and we were still on top of the hills making guard, protecting the folks so everyone could get out. And we could see them [PVA forces] on some of the hills about two miles [3.2 km] away, approaching. On that day, they call[ed] us and they told us to come down to the port and leave everything behind except your weapon and . . . whatever ammunition you have left. . . . Destroy whatever you can. We got to the port and there was a lot of railroad cars and vehicles loaded with ammunition, food, gasoline, all kinds of supplies, and they had dynamite charges already set in place, and they told us to be careful not to trip over them.

After they loaded onto the final ship and set sail, the dynamite detonated. The soldiers looked back and watched the port explode. The buildings, the vehicles, the train cars—everything—erupted in smoke and flame.

Historians have called the retreat out of Hungnam the greatest evacuation movement by sea in US military history. In only three weeks, the Borinqueneers had assisted in the evacuation of 105,000 soldiers, 17,500 vehicles, and 350,000 tons (317,515 t) of supplies, all under heavy enemy fire. The service and heroism of the 65th was recognized back on the United States mainland. The *Charleston Gazette* wrote,

> One of the most cheering reports coming from the recent evacuation of our troops from Hungnam Beachhead is that which has to do with the actions of the 65th Infantry Regiment. From all reports this regiment distinguished itself above and beyond the call of duty in the bitter fighting which preserved the beachhead and made possible the redeployment of the X Corps which had been isolated in Northwest Korea. The men of the 65th Infantry Regiment are . . . worthy of all of the fine things that have been said about [them]. The only difference between this regiment and others is that they are native Puerto Ricans. . . . A salute to American fighting men—especially the 65th Infantry Regiment.

They respected and believed in their leaders. Their leaders respected them. Their training paid off. The heroic and lifesaving acts of the Borinqueneers earned them great praise at home and within the military. Their generals and fellow soldiers recognized their bravery and service.

Photographers aboard the evacuating ships captured the explosion that destroyed Hungnam's port.

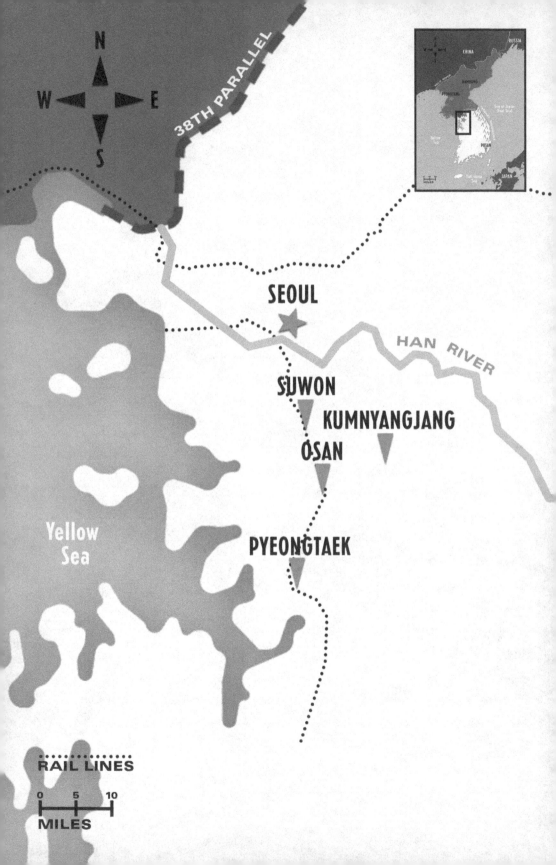

CHAPTER 6
Retaking Seoul

Self-reliance, stamina, courage, and bravery were characteristic of all of the Puerto Ricans of the 65th.

—Brigadier General W. W. Harris (Ret.)

The Borinqueneers arrived back in Pusan on New Year's Day 1951. The soldiers had a few days of rest and relaxation. They took much-needed showers. For some soldiers, it had been months since they had a shower. They shaved and trimmed the beards that had become unruly during the fighting up north and ate hot meals. In Pusan they restocked ammunition as well as fixed and replaced their equipment.

But their rest was brief. After the successful evacuation, the PVA had advanced into South Korea and captured its capital, Seoul. The 65th Infantry was directed to push north, retake Seoul, and drive the PVA all the way back to the Yalu River on the border of China. By January 5, 1951, they were once again sent out from Pusan to the front lines.

From Pusan they traveled to the north, fighting along the way in Pyeongtaek, Osan, and Kumnyangjang. Just south of the city of

Suwon, the 65th Infantry's G Company was ordered to attack several hills held by PVA forces in January. They succeeded in taking the hills, but the enemy soon counterattacked with even greater numbers. The G Company was overrun and the leaders, Corporal Gonzalez S. Centeno and Sergeant Alfonso Garcia, were captured, along with fourteen other soldiers.

The captured men were taken to the enemy's command post and questioned by one of the Chinese officers. After a long interrogation, the officer told them he was not happy with their answers. "One of the soldiers hit me in the head with his rifle," Garcia later recalled. The impact knocked him out. "I do not remember how long I was unconscious."

When Garcia awoke, he and Centeno were forced to march every night for up to twelve hours. There were sixteen of them, eight British soldiers and eight GIs. One night one of the soldiers from the 65th stumbled, too weak to keep walking. A PVA soldier was ordered to stay behind with him as the column continued forward. After some time, a shot rang out in the hills. The guard returned to the column, alone.

Garcia and Centeno knew they had to escape if they were going to make it out alive. They decided the best chance they had was to escape during a UNC air raid. The UNC forces had greater control over the air so they would drop bombs from planes to slow the enemy down from advancing their position. One night, as the imprisoned soldiers and their PVA guards were hunkered down under cover from the dropping bombs, the soldiers made a break for it. They kicked in the door of the hut they were held in and ran for the nearest hill. Shots rang out behind them, but they sprinted on. Soon they lost their guards in the dark of night. They were free.

But their situation was still dire. During the day they had to hide from nearby PVA patrols. At night they traveled as far south as they could, entirely on foot, through the cold mountains. After several nights, it began to snow heavily, making it hard to find their way.

Former prisoners of war huddle around a stove to warm themselves after being returned to the UNC. After the end of the Korean War, many American POWs would remain unaccounted for.

A patrol of Borinqueneers captured enemy troops near Yonghung and led them back to camp to hold them as prisoners of war. Some seven thousand POWs from North Korea and China would die in the UNC camps, most due to tuberculosis and dysentery.

So the soldiers walked during the day and rested at night. Eventually, they reached a river. Exhausted and surrounded by the enemy, they had no other option but to cross it. Centeno, however, did not know how to swim, so Garcia had to carry him across.

Soaking wet, shivering, and barely able to walk, they sheltered in a cave for a few days until they heard a nearby PVA patrol coming their way. They moved out, hoping to run into Allied forces before they succumbed to frostbite. Luckily, it was only a few days before they ran into a small patrol of South Korean soldiers, who loaded them into vehicles. Two months after their capture, the soldiers of G Company were reunited with the rest of the 65th. Aside from the man who had been shot by the PVA, they had all survived.

While the soldiers of the G Company were marching as prisoners of war, the rest of the 65th faced intense fighting as they advanced to Seoul. During the day, they marched, encountering surprisingly little resistance. As evening fell, the soldiers found some high ground to set up camp for the night. But every morning before sunrise, like clockwork, they were attacked. Enemy soldiers hid in the surrounding hills watching the movements of US forces during the day, waiting until the darkest point of the night to advance toward them and strike. And each night, the number of enemy troops increased. Undeterred, the 65th pressed on. Their progress north was steady but slow. They were encountering PVA forces more often. They were approaching the main line of resistance.

By early January, the 65th had received news that Walker had been killed in a jeep accident. Lieutenant General Matthew B. Ridgway had replaced Walker as the commander of the 8th Army. In World War II, Ridgway had been the first commanding general of the 82nd "All American" Airborne Division, with whom he parachuted into Normandy, and later the XVIII Airborne Corps. He was known for wearing a hand grenade strapped to one shoulder and a first aid kit on the other.

MacArthur allowed Ridgway a lot of flexibility with the command of the 8th Army, and Ridgway used it. He did not support the old segregation policies of the army. He believed it was "un-American . . . for free citizens to be taught to downgrade themselves this way as if they were unfit to associate with their fellows or accept leadership themselves."

As commander of the 8th Army, Ridgway was Harris's commanding officer. For two days he stayed with Harris and the 65th, watching as the unit attacked and captured two hills from the enemy in just one day. Ridgway was impressed by their teamwork, efficiency, and coolness in battle. He directed the commander of the 3rd Infantry Division to assign the replacements being trained at Camp Tortuguero to the entire 3rd Infantry Division, not just within the 65th Infantry Regiment. That meant Puerto Rican soldiers would fight alongside white soldiers as part of the same unit for the first time.

Fighting was particularly tough from Suwon to the Han River just south of Seoul. As they pushed PVA forces back north, the 65th Infantry encountered heavier mortar and artillery fire. Intense explosions from the constant shelling surrounded them. Using their own artillery, the 65th focused on attacking their enemy's guns. After successfully destroying the source of the shelling, the 65th stormed the hills where the enemy was hiding with rifles and grenades, driving them out.

On February 9, after nearly a month of marching and fighting their way north, they reached a hill overlooking the Han River. They could see the snowy mountains on the other side of the winter landscape. There, with Seoul in sight, the men of the 65th were finally able to rest. Relieved from combat by the 15th Infantry, the Borinqueneers found three hills behind the front lines. They set up camp, each battalion setting up on a different hill. The command post was set up in the flat valley between them.

A group of five Borinqueneers formed a quintet called the Sons of Puerto Rico and sang songs from their homeland to their fellow soldiers. *Left to right:* Privates Jose Figueroa, Sonny Rivera Maldonado (*back*), Carlos Paul Melendez, Enrique Roque Ortiz, and Rafael Rivera Rodriquez.

C rations were very limited in selection but provided necessary nourishment for troops when fresh and prepared food was unavailable.

Happy not to be on the front lines, the 65th enjoyed what was the best meal they could ask for on the battlefield: precooked C rations, hard biscuits, beans, and awful-tasting coffee. They also indulged in sponge baths, which might sound luxurious, but in reality, each soldier had just a helmet full of water, a bar of soap, a towel, and a toothbrush.

They played Puerto Rican music on portable phonographs they had brought with them overseas, and some soldiers played the instruments they had brought with them. One soldier, Corporal Juan Landrau, captured a bugle from the PVA that he sent to the governor of Puerto Rico as a souvenir.

For the battlefield, this was lavish. Around then the soldiers also received new sleeping bags made with down and a quick open cord that made it easier to spring into action when attacked. That night they happily went to bed, comfortable and with full bellies.

That night the 65th awoke to the sounds of explosions. *Ka-Boom! Ka-BOOM! KA-BOOM! Whizz! Whizz!* "What was that?" Harris woke up thinking. "The way it sounded it wouldn't take long before the entire staff . . . would all be dead or captured." *BOOM! BOOM!* The bombing continued. It was the NKPA.

Famous Frogs

The national animal of Puerto Rico is the coqui (pronounced *ko-kee*). Unlike most other tree frogs, the coqui does not have webbed feet. The tiny frog is about 1 to 2 inches (2.5 to 5 cm) long and usually brown, yellow, or green. The melodic choruses of male coqui frogs can be heard throughout Puerto Rico from dusk to dawn. The seventeen species of coqui in Puerto Rico are found mostly in the El Yunque National Forest. The whistling frog's ballads are featured in some Puerto Rican poems and in numerous songs.

Harris immediately called the battalion commanders, ordering them to move out from their hills and attempt to surround the enemy.

The soldiers executed the plan perfectly. By daybreak, the explosions ended, and the enemy retreated. After the dust settled and they cleaned the soot from their eyes, the Borinqueneers saw that they had lost one soldier and that six others were wounded. But their intensity and focus on the battlefield led to over eight hundred NKPA soldiers either captured or killed.

When he heard of the quick response of the 65th Infantry to the sudden attack, Soule, the commander of the 3rd Division, wrote in a letter commending them for their work, "I am proud of you and the division's record on this occasion. . . . The cooperation and fighting spirit [you have] shown will assure us of victory over our enemies." The 65th regularly received letters like this and heard of articles praising their fighting ability and spirit. Puerto Rico's legislature also approved a resolution of support and thankfulness "to the men of the 65th Infantry Regiment for their heroic tasks on the battlefields of the Korean peninsula in defense of the principles of democracy."

The regiment's rest only lasted a few days. On February 12 to 16, portions of the regiment were fighting again. The enemy usually attacked in the wee hours of the morning, but the Borinqueneers pushed them back each time.

Around noon on February 17, a line of over twenty jeeps came barreling down the dirt road. While still seated in his jeep, MacArthur, the commander in chief of UNC forces, approached Harris, looking crisp and formidable in his standard aviator glasses, buttoned-up khaki jumpsuit, and tan army hat. As Harris recalled later, he "walked up to the jeep, saluted him and the first thing he said to me was 'Are your troops still doing the same fine job they have been?'"

The rare sight of the five-star general caught the soldiers' attention, and his approval of their conduct filled them with pride. Hundreds of soldiers circled nearby as Harris briefed MacArthur on the current situation, straining to hear what the two officers were talking about. Finally, Harris saluted the general, and off MacArthur went with the line of jeeps. Everyone else picked their jaws up off the ground, caught their breath, and then went back to work.

As February turned into March, the weather began to warm, melting the ice and snow and creating swampy ponds on the roads. But at night, the temperature dropped below freezing again, covering everything in sheets of ice once more. This forced the 8th Army to postpone the river

Soldiers cross the Han River as part of the offensive to retake Seoul.

crossing. They stayed on the bank of the Han River well into March.

By February 20, the 65th were still south of the Han River, looking across to Seoul. The US military and the rest of the UNC forces were preparing to retake Seoul from the Chinese and North Korean forces. They were going to cross the river and strike the enemy forces head-on as part of a huge offensive.

While the Borinqueneers trained and prepared to cross the river, the soldiers on the right flank fought the enemy. Ridgway strategized to circle the Chinese troops. Once the Chinese realized that the circle was forming around them, they quickly retreated from Seoul.

On March 12, spy planes noticed six hundred North Korean and Chinese soldiers walking away from Seoul toward the northwest.

On March 16, the 65th Infantry's 2nd Battalion crossed the Han River and entered Seoul. The following day, they continued north to fight the enemy so the rest of the regiment could cross. They made it 5,000 yards (4,570 m) and could not find the enemy. That day the 1st Battalion joined them, and on March 18 the last of the 65th Infantry entered the city. By spring of 1951, the United States and their allies had fully recaptured Seoul for the last time.

> By spring of 1951, the United States and their allies had fully recaptured Seoul for the last time.

N
W — E
S

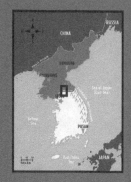

PYONGGANG

CHORWON   IRON   KUMHWA   38TH PARALLEL
                TRIANGLE

0   2.5   5
MILES

CHAPTER 7
Seesaw Operations

The Puerto Ricans forming the ranks of the gallant 65th Infantry give daily proof on the battlefields of Korea of their courage, determination and resolute will to victory, their invincible loyalty to the United States and their fervent devotion to those immutable principles of human relations which the Americans of the continent and Puerto Rico have in common. They are writing a brilliant record of heroism in battle.

—General Douglas MacArthur

Seoul had been recaptured for the South Korean government, but for MacArthur the war was far from won. He wanted to eliminate the Communist government from North Korea, uniting it with South Korea under a capitalist government. He also wanted to attack China for supporting North Korea.

To achieve this goal, MacArthur pushed Truman and his Joint Chiefs of Staff to authorize the use of nuclear weapons. But Truman was hesitant to allow MacArthur to launch nuclear strikes on North Korea. The world had been shocked and horrified by the destructive power of

In December 1951 the PVA pushed the 65th Infantry Regiment to retreat south of the town of Oro-ri. The bridge burning in the background was destroyed by the retreating soldiers, who then took up a post across the river, keeping guard against opposing forces.

the bombs used to attack the Japanese cities of Hiroshima and Nagasaki in 1945. Truman also did not want to push the Soviet Union, which was allied with China, to use nuclear weapons in response, launching a global nuclear war. Despite these worries, Truman arranged to send nine Mark IV nuclear capsules to the air force's 9th Bomb Squadron.

Meanwhile, Truman was becoming increasingly concerned with how MacArthur was handling the war. After the recapture of Seoul, US forces failed to push Chinese and North Korean forces far past the 38th parallel. Instead, they had been forced into an orderly retreat toward Seoul. Truman began to discuss the possibility of ending the war without taking North Korea. He wanted to broker a peace deal even if it meant the North Korean government would remain Communist and therefore separate from the government in South Korea. He thought if they preserved the US-allied government in South Korea and maintained the dividing line of the 38th parallel, they could leave Korea without risking more American lives and prevent the Soviet Union from gaining more global power.

But MacArthur refused to abandon North Korea. As he pushed Truman and UN leaders to escalate the war and begin bombing closer and closer to the Chinese border, world leaders began to question MacArthur's leadership. Finally, enough was enough. Truman removed MacArthur in April 1951, replacing him with Ridgway. James A. Van Fleet was promoted to lieutenant general and given command of the 8th Army.

After MacArthur arrived in the United States, he was asked to testify before Congress about his leadership of the Korean War to determine if his removal had been authorized under the powers of the presidency. MacArthur spoke for six hours during the beginning of the seven weeks of congressional hearings. MacArthur claimed his actions had been supported by the Joint Chiefs of Staff, the most senior uniformed leaders of the US Department of Defense. But the Joint Chiefs of Staff contradicted this, instead claiming that MacArthur's strategy would have eventually pulled the United States into a larger war in Asia. The committee found that Truman acted within the presidential powers, and his dismissal of MacArthur was upheld.

That April the 65th were in what Harris called "seesaw operations." They were ordered back and forth across the 38th parallel. It was north of the line that Cartagena charged Hill 206, single-handedly destroying enemy emplacements one by one and allowing the 65th to take an additional two hills nearby. But they were soon met by such fierce resistance that they were forced to make an orderly withdrawal back to Seoul. The enemy continued to fight them and the other UNC forces the whole way back to the 38th parallel.

The Chinese were increasing their forces in the region. With constant enemy pressure, the 3rd Division was ordered to retreat to Seoul on April 27. The Borinqueneers were directed to send two battalions to assist in the extraction of the 25th US Infantry Division. The rest of the regiment was ordered into a blocking position behind a brigade of British soldiers to defend their retreat to Seoul. Harris wanted to ensure that the Borinqueneers were not surrounded by the enemy and trapped as they protected the 3rd Division's retreat. By the end of April, they were just outside of Seoul behind other UNC forces. There, they dug in, creating temporary fortifications such as foxholes, command posts, and connecting trenches similar to those that they had built in Vieques during Operation PORTREX. They protected these fortifications with

A UNC bomb destroys North Korean supplies in the city of Wonsan. The Siege of Wonsan, during which UNC forces prevented North Korean forces from using the city's port, is the longest naval blockade in history.

barbed wire. Harris also prepared counterattack plans if the enemy broke through the main lines. The PVA must not reach Seoul.

The army's experience from World War II showed army leaders that replacing troops after long periods of combat increased their spirits and made them better soldiers. The 8th Army had implemented a troop rotation policy in August 1950. The goal was to rotate out commanders and soldiers before they would succumb to what commanders called "battle exhaustion." The soldiers who spent the most time on the front lines were given priority for rotation to allow them to rest and recover before returning to combat.

According to military historian Colonel Gilberto Villahermosa, "a soldier would be eligible for rotation after he spent six months with a combat division or smaller unit in Korea, twelve months in Korea with a support unit, or any combination of the two."

Puerto Ricans were 60 percent of the replacement soldiers scheduled to arrive in Korea in April 1951. An additional twenty-three hundred Puerto Rican soldiers were also in transit to Korea. Given the policy and Ridgway's beliefs about integration, the replacement soldiers were sent to the 65th as well as other units in the 3rd Infantry Division.

By mid-May, the 65th was moving north again. They found the enemy tired and were able to push right through them. The Borinqueneers had suffered eleven combat casualties in May, but they had killed over four hundred enemy soldiers, captured eighty-one, and seized stockpiles of ammunition along with Russian-made artillery. But though the enemy was tired, so were the Borinqueneers. Many soldiers were ready for rotation.

> Though the enemy was tired, so were the Borinqueneers. Many soldiers were ready for rotation.

In May 1951, some seven hundred soldiers, almost 20 percent of the unit's strength, was rotated back to the United States, boosting morale among the remaining soldiers. But the rotated soldiers were replaced by only nine officers and 155 new enlisted soldiers. At this point, the only original battalion commander that sailed from Puerto Rico in August 1950 was St. Clair. He remained along with Harris.

The Iron Triangle, located between the three towns of Chorwon, Kumhwa, and Pyonggang, was a key strategic region for Chinese and North Korean forces. The region contained some of the most important road and rail connections between the port of Wonsan and Seoul.

The unit did not have much time to orient new personnel. In early June, the 65th were closing in on the Iron Triangle. But the fighting changed. Instead of large battles involving the whole 65th Infantry Division, most of the fighting happened in intense and bloody battles between small units and companies.

During the first half of June, 11 inches (28 cm) of rain fell, causing rivers to rise and flood huge parts of Korea. The 65th Infantry Regiment was losing soldiers to drownings as well as enemy fire. The enemy defended their area during the day and counterattacked at night. The 65th continued to fight to secure their main line of resistance toward Chorwon.

On June 16, Harris received reassignment. He had commanded the 65th Infantry for over two years, longer than most commanders went without being reassigned. The news made him "a bit emotional" but he knew that it was time for him to leave.

In the end of June, the 65th received more bad news. From a combination of deaths, injuries, and rotations, the number of soldiers in the unit dropped to the lowest it had ever reached during the Korean War. To increase the number of troops, Soule, the 3rd Division commander, had to make tough choices. He transferred some of the Puerto Rican soldiers who were fighting in integrated units into the segregated 65th Infantry Regiment. The 8th Army promised

> Morale was low, but the exhausted soldiers who had been in combat for several months rallied to help train the new inexperienced soldiers.

him 250 new recruits per month. Finally, Soule halted rotations back to the United States. Even if they met the criteria for rotation, Soule's decision forced them to stay in Korea. These steps increased the number of soldiers in the unit to 3,780 in early July. It was still below their authorized strength level. Morale was low, but the exhausted soldiers who had been in combat for several months rallied to help train the new inexperienced soldiers and continued to improve their defensive positions along the main line of resistance.

St. Clair, the last of the original battalion commanders who sailed from Puerto Rico in the summer of 1950, was finally rotated back to the United States in July 1951. The 65th had lost Harris and all three original battalion commanders within three months. The loss of experienced

Colonel William W. Harris (*left*) speaks with Major General William H. Turner, whose air force pilots flew the C-47s that dropped supplies to the 2nd Battalion. From his experience leading the 65th Infantry Regiment for several years, Harris came to deeply respect the Puerto Rican soldiers.

Borinqueneer Manhandles MG
to Keep Red Lying Low

While defending Hill 476 near Uijongbu, Korea, Corporal Armando Rosa found himself and his troops surrounded by PVA forces. An article from the *Front Line*, the newspaper of the 3rd Division, provided an account of what happened next:

> The Hollywood style of shooting a thirty-caliber machine gun from the hip may not always be practical, but [Corporal] Armando Rosa of D Company, 65th Infantry has found it quite effective.
>
> The corporal, attached to elements of B and C Company during a recent Chinese attack, used this method of keeping the enemy from breathing down the necks of the Puerto Ricans as they effected an orderly withdrawal.
>
> On a foggy morning the enemy attacked near Rosa's position at the forward point of the defense line. Rosa leaped up from his hole, firing from the hip, and backed from the enemy with the gun blazing. He crossed two ridges in this manner, keeping the Chinese forward movement at a slow crawl. He enabled the rest of his company to take up defensive positions by his action. No accurate account of the enemy killed by Rosa is available, but he fired a total of 3,500 rounds by himself, and all from the hip.

As they advance into the Iron Triangle, Borinqueneers seek cover in a trench that had been dug by PVA soldiers and captured by UNC forces.

leaders and the rotation out of experienced combat troops hit the 65th Infantry Regiment hard. Forty experienced officers and 1,244 sergeants and enlisted soldiers left Korea. The unit lost a third of its approved strength from rotation alone.

Soule wrote in his monthly command report that "the shortage of Puerto Rican replacements remains a problem. Unless replacements for combat arms officers also arrive, it is quite possible a serious morale problem will arise." And the replacements soldiers had only basic training, not the extensive training and instruction the previous Borinqueneers had.

N
W E
S

IMJIN RIVER

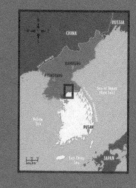

PYONGGANG

JACKSON HEIGHTS

CHORWON **IRON TRIANGLE** KUMHWA

OUTPOST KELLY

38TH PARALLEL

0 2.5 5
MILES

CHAPTER 8
Outpost Kelly

The war changed complexion from being a war of movement . . . it became a war of fixed positions, and it became static."

—Lieutenant Colonel William A. Friedman

In mid-July, the fighting seemed to slow. By then the Communists suffered five hundred thousand casualties, but the front lines had hardly moved. Since the spring of 1951, Truman wanted to negotiate a truce and a cease-fire. When MacArthur would not agree, Truman had replaced him. In July 1951, formal peace talks began between the UNC forces and the Communist forces in Kaesong, north of the 38th parallel line. Later talks moved to Panmunjom. But the talks stalled. The Korean War took center stage during the race for the US presidency, where Republican candidate Dwight D. Eisenhower criticized Truman's handling of the war. The war was also very unpopular among the US public.

By August the 65th were moving north toward Pyonggang under constant, heavy rain. The rain washed away roads and bridges, and river levels rose, threatening to flood the Iron Triangle.

In September the 65th was ordered to gain positions on a ridgeline outside of Chorwon. On the morning of the mission, thick, dense fog obscured their surroundings and inhibited their progress. Once the fog lifted, a torrential rain began to fall. They heard the crack of enemy fire in the distance. They tried to proceed, but sudden and intense enemy resistance stopped them. The strength of the enemy forces shocked them. Enemy combatants had seemed to emerge from nowhere, as if they were ghosts in the fog. The weather had made maneuvering the tanks difficult, and when the tanks finally found some traction, they set off unexpected explosions: land mines.

The 65th realized that the enemy had taken advantage of the relatively slow fighting during the summer peace talks to occupy, organize, and fortify new regions. They had hidden and covered communications trenches and foxholes as well as caves for shelter and supplies. They had also buried mines and booby traps in areas where the UNC forces were likely to approach. Soule and Colonel Erwin O. Gibson, who had replaced Harris, were surprised by how well prepared the enemy was. As soon as they received reports of the intensity of the forces pressing against the 65th, they ordered them to retreat and try another route.

Meanwhile, another hero emerged from the Borinqueneers. When the troops were pushed back, Master Sergeant Pedro Zayas urged the men to keep fighting. Exposing himself to enemy fire, he pushed forward to solidify the defense line. Though wounded and close to the enemy, he devastated them with machine-gun fire and by lobbing grenade after grenade. When he later received the Silver Star, Zayas was commended for his "gallant and effective leadership [that] reflects the highest credit upon himself and the military services."

Fighting against both the weather and their entrenched enemy, the Borinqueneers slowly advanced farther into the Iron Triangle, eventually reaching positions 5 miles (8 km) north of the 38th parallel, which had marked the front lines for much of the war. On top of facing heavy fire the whole way north, they were still beleaguered by the rotation policy.

Soldiers disarm a booby trap laid by the opposing forces.

The commanders were struggling to find enough replacement soldiers to rotate into the conflict, and some six hundred soldiers eligible for rotation could not leave Korea. The new soldiers lacked the same degree of training and combat experience of the men they had replaced. The soldiers in the early part of the war were generally long-term volunteers who bonded and knew one another for a while. The replacement soldiers did not have the same personal bonds, let alone combat experience. By September 1951, the unit's numbers had fallen to 3,678, below their authorized minimum of 3,686. Meanwhile, the 17th and 15th Infantry each had around 4,000 soldiers.

In November, while peace talks took place, Ridgway directed military units to only hold the main line of resistance. Even though they would come under intense fire from the enemy, they were to use only enough firepower to keep the enemy from advancing. If the UNC forces tried to advance, their actions could undermine the peace negotiations and prolong the war.

The 65th had to stop, dig in their heels, and endure a constant barrage of fire from the enemy. Experienced soldiers who were overdue for rotation were exhausted, and new soldiers were unprepared for the intensity of the combat. Holding the main line of resistance was a test of determination and will, two qualities the Borinqueneers had in abundance. But even they were beginning to suffer a loss of morale. As military historian Villahermosa said in *Honor and Fidelity: The 65th Infantry in Korea, 1950–1953*, "During the first six months of 1952, the 65th Infantry lost a total of 5,297 soldiers (either casualties or rotations) and gained 3,825." The number of new soldiers to the unit was nearly the same as that of men that originally sailed from Puerto Rico in 1950.

> Holding the main line of resistance was a test of determination and will, two qualities the Borinqueneers had in abundance. But even they were beginning to suffer a loss of morale.

3RD INFANTRY DIVISION

	65th Infantry	7th Infantry	15th Infantry
Days in battle	460	424	419
Losses (battle and nonbattle)	4,330	5,227	4,524
Taken enemy prisoners*	2,133	595	1,076

*Enemy prisoners, or prisoners of war, were Communist soldiers who the UNC forces captured while fighting.

Neither side advanced much through the winter. But in February 1952, some change occurred: Colonel Juan Cordero Dávila became the commander of the 65th. Unlike previous commanders, Cordero Dávila came from the Puerto Rican National Guard. He was a veteran of World War II, where he was battalion commander and later a regimental executive officer in the 65th Regiment. He had extensive administrative and staffing experience. But he did not have the battlefield experience and formal military education of Harris.

Many of the Borinqueneers were familiar with Cordero Dávila, since two-thirds of the 65th Regiment had trained under him as part of the 296th Regimental Combat Team in Puerto Rico before coming to Korea. Once he arrived in Korea, Cordero Dávila ordered the men to do various training exercises and equipment inspections. Some of the weapons and equipment inspections were exhaustive and took away time from much-needed tactical and coordination training. But Cordero Dávila brought the unit's vehicles, kitchen supplies, weapons, and staff files up to acceptable standards.

Despite Cordero Dávila's new training regimen, the messy rotation schedule made it difficult to build trained capacity in the regiment. Many of the most experienced personnel were rotated out of the unit quicker than new personnel could be trained. Over the course of the year they also lost their noncommissioned officers, the bilingual connection between the English-speaking officers and the Spanish-speaking enlisted soldiers, in rotation.

Many of the Puerto Rican soldiers rotated to Korea did not speak English, and many were sent to units other than the 65th Infantry Regiment. In 1951, for example, twelve hundred Puerto Rican replacement soldiers were rotated to Korea, but only four hundred were assigned to the 65th. Many Puerto Rican soldiers found it difficult to work with the English-speaking soldiers. That meant they were even less effective on the field. Cordero Dávila explained in his August 1952 monthly report, "The inability to express [himself] easily creates in the Puerto Rican soldier hardship in his performance of duty. In a Spanish-speaking unit the Puerto Rican soldier sheds his handicap and enjoys a feeling of equality in competing with his fellow soldiers. Also, he performs his duties with more confidence since there is no question of misinterpretation or misunderstanding." And these newer soldiers had

A machine gun team from the 65th Infantry Regiment engages in an exchange with enemy troops, who have taken up a post in nearby hilltops. Machine gun teams consist of a gunner, an assistant gunner, and an ammunition bearer. Two machine gun teams make up a weapon squad.

even less experience as they were new volunteers or draftees. They came to Korea with only a couple of months of basic training.

By the fall of 1952, Chinese forces became much more aggressive in their attacks, especially on high ridges and hills. They forced the 8th Army into a stalemate, holding its position but unable to push farther north.

As the war stalled, hostilities brewed within the 65th Infantry. A shower was built for the regimental staff, but Lieutenant Colonel Clayton C. Craig, a white officer from the United States, ordered that no Puerto Ricans could use the shower, even though several of the officers were Puerto Rican. The commander of the 2nd Battalion, Colonel Carlos Betances Ramírez, as the unit's executive officer, took a shower anyway.

Reduced personnel with less experience, less bilingual communication links, failing morale, and racial hostilities between officers and enlisted soldiers contributed to the disasters that were to come in the months of September and October 1952. The Borinqueneers were about to face their toughest battles yet, and they were not prepared.

The Borinqueneers were about to face their toughest battles yet, and they were not prepared.

On September 18, 1952, the 65th Infantry's B Company relieved C Company from their position of defending Outpost Kelly. Outpost Kelly stood on a ridge about a mile (1.6 km) west of the Imjin River, which flowed south past the 38th parallel to join the Han River near Seoul. Outpost Kelly had sleeping bunkers, a small command bunker, an outer circle of automatic weapons bunkers, and a circular trench at the top of the hill.

Around nine thirty at night, the officers inside the command bunker were planning their next moves when they heard small arms gun fire outside. This was not unusual so close to the front lines, and they continued with their briefing. Suddenly, the small wooden door flung open and multiple grenades smacked onto the floor. One commander was close enough to the door to make it past the threshold when the grenades exploded, catapulting him through the air. He landed on the ground right in front of a group of Chinese soldiers with machine guns. He immediately leaped to his feet, ignoring the pain blazing from his wounded leg, and fled down the hill.

Less than an hour later, Chinese forces controlled Outpost Kelly. They had killed or captured many of the soldiers on the hill. The rest of the 65th, who were holding the main line of resistance below the hill, could see from below their fellow soldiers who were captured. Assessments revealed that 40 percent of B Company had been killed, was wounded, or was missing because of the surprise attack.

Shocked by the surprise attack, Cordero Dávila knew he had to think carefully about his response. To the surprise of many of his men, he did not immediately order them to recapture the hill. As First Lieutenant Duquesne Wolf later wrote, "There was a reluctance on the part of the

Regiment and Division to begin shelling the enemy for fear of killing our own troops." While they waited, the Chinese fortified their positions by adding more firepower to the hill in case UNC forces tried to take it back.

Finally, Cordero Dávila decided Outpost Kelly could not be left in enemy hands. Over the next few days, his men tried over and over again to retake the hill. But over and over again they failed. They tried to send smaller groups of soldiers to determine the strength of the Chinese group. Within three hours, that group was dragging their wounded soldiers back to their original locations. They determined that about one hundred Chinese soldiers had the hill. They requested air strikes, but were denied out of fear for the wounded UNC soldiers lying on the hill. Just before midnight on September 21, they tried again. But the barrage of enemy fire stopped them. They made another attempt just before five that morning. The heavy enemy fire stopped them again. The sieges were bloody and violent. Grenades and gunfire destroyed what remained of the natural ground cover and left many more soldiers dead. Former soldier Eugenio Martinez Matos recalled, "It looked . . . as if there had never been any vegetation there. That's how the hill looked. There were pieces of legs with shoes. . . . It was a very traumatic experience."

After the 65th's multiple failed attempts, Lieutenant General Paul W. Kendall of the I Corps came to Cordero Dávila's aid. After their stern discussion, Cordero Dávila organized the men to try to retake the hill again, this time with additional resources from other units. But they failed again. Soldier Sergio Lopez de Lopez recounted, "Thirty-eight men went up. Three came down."

"Thirty-eight men went up. Three came down."

By September 25 the 3rd Division finally ended the assault on Outpost Kelly. The outpost was left under enemy control.

During September 1952, the 65th Infantry Regiment had sustained 413 casualties from battle, and 352 of them had occurred at Outpost Kelly alone. This was the highest number of casualties the 65th had suffered in a single battle in Korea since they arrived two years ago.

Eric Cestero (*front*) of Bayamon, Puerto Rico, kneels to pray with other members of the 65th Infantry Regiment during a memorial mass on the front lines. The mass honored the soldiers who had been killed in the war so far. For many who went on to try to take Outpost Kelly from PVA control, it would be their last mass.

At Outpost Kelly, Borinqueneers carry a wounded comrade back behind the front lines so he can receive medical attention. There were so many wounded casualties lying on the hillside that it prevented the commanders from calling an air strike, which might have turned the tide of the battle.

Captain Willis Cronkhite, an officer of the 65th Infantry Regiment, later remembered the bravery of his men in the face of a hopeless assault. "When I came off of Kelly Hill, one of my sergeants came to me and requested permission to go to the aid station. . . . He showed me his wound. And there were maggots in it. I said, 'Why didn't you go to aid station as soon as you were shot?' Because it obviously had been days. He said, 'I was the only one who knew how to adjust artillery fire. . . . I felt I needed to stay and help my comrades in that tight situation. . . .' Those men were so incredibly brave. It's just unbelievable."

Higher-ranking army officials blamed the failure to recapture Outpost Kelly on Cordero Dávila's lack of combat experience and inability to execute combat maneuvers. They also faulted General

Robert L. Dulaney, the 3rd Infantry Division commander, for making poor decisions and missing details due to his stubbornness and vanity. Dulaney was replaced by General George Smythe while Cordero Dávila resigned as the commander of the 65th Infantry Regiment and returned to Puerto Rico. Colonel Chester DeGavre, a Spanish-speaking officer from the mainland United States, replaced him. The Borinqueneers had lost their only Puerto Rican unit commander.

But DeGavre already had experience leading the regiment, having served as one of its commanders from 1937 to 1939. Because of his history with the unit, he immediately noticed that things were different. He was concerned by the language divide and lack of NCOs And after the horrendous and traumatic events at Outpost Kelly, the young enlisted soldiers had become nervous and jumpy. They fired into the darkness and threw grenades at every sound from the main defensive line.

DeGavre believed the solution to this was more discipline. He thought if he brought more stability and order to the regiment, the soldiers' morale would return. So DeGavre made a controversial decision. He ordered the 65th to cut their hair, mustaches, and beards. "Until such a time as they gave proof of their manhood," he added.

The soldiers were shocked and offended. Mustaches were very important to Puerto Rican men. As Major Silvestre E. Ortiz wrote, "It is part of [a Puerto Rican man's] personality, in many cases the product of a religious vow, so much so that three chaplains went to visit [DeGavre] and appraised him of its importance, unsuccessfully." For the Puerto Rican soldiers, placing doubt on their manhood was the ultimate insult. Betances Ramírez objected to the order, but DeGavre did not sway.

DeGavre also ordered the removal of their battle name, the Borinqueneers, from the 65th's vehicles and ended the inclusion of traditional Puerto Rican dishes, such as rice and beans, from their army-issued food rations. But none of this had the effect he intended. Morale sank even further as the 65th Infantry Regiment approached its greatest challenge.

CHAPTER 9
Jackson Heights

It was a contemptible, worthless piece of ground; ill-formed by nature for all-around defense. . . . The outpost was a solid rock—no chance for fortifications . . . we could not dig trenches; men had to lie on the ground behind rocks. Every move was detected by an invisible enemy. . . . [The] enemy had concealment and cover we had none.

—Lieutenant Colonel George Jackson

During early and mid-October, the 65th conducted training exercises to try to address the failures of Kelly Hill. Initially, they did not have live ammunition to conduct the trainings. Without the live ammunition, the exercises lacked realism. Once they received ammunition, their training period was extended to allow for more realistic training exercises. But at the end of the training, Jackson said that the men still "needed more time to select and [instruct] untrained personnel for supervisory duties of NCOs."

While they were in reserve training, the fighting was still intense. The 8th Army pushed forward to gain hills and ridges in the Iron

Triangle. After several days of fierce fighting, the UNC gained some of the hills, but they knew that the Chinese would be back to try to regain those hills. One of those was Hill 391.

Hill 391 was an outpost about 2,000 yards (1,830 m) north of the main line of resistance, in Chinese-held territory, and beyond the range of most US heavy artillery support. Resupplying the outpost was extremely difficult because it was under constant observation by the enemy. And the hill of hard, solid rock was especially hard to defend. There was no dirt to dig in to build defensive emplacements. The men defending Hill 391 were sitting ducks.

The men defending Hill 391 were sitting ducks.

At the end of October, G Company of the 2nd Battalion was ordered to relieve soldiers on Hill 391 and defend the hill. The hill would later be called Jackson Heights after G Company's commander.

On October 25 at eleven in the morning, the Chinese soldiers began firing incessantly at Hill 391 from a nearby ridge, continuing all day and into the night. G Company took cover and fired some flares back to keep the enemy from charging the hill. But late that night, the Chinese forces began to flank the outpost from the east and west. G Company stood strong and pushed them back but sustained many casualties. The 65th held their position after repeated assaults through the following day.

On the morning of October 27, the enemy tried again, firing "rounds . . . from every direction," Betances Ramírez recalled.

They destroyed 75 percent of G Company's ammunition supply, and by the afternoon at least a dozen men were injured and several lay dead from the relentless shelling. The remaining men fired round after round and mortar after mortar, but the number of casualties skyrocketed. By evening Betances Ramírez ordered the men to withdraw. "It was horrible. There were rounds landing three and four at a time. It was everywhere," he later recalled.

The next day, DeGavre ordered the men to retake Hill 391 with two groups: A Company and F Company. F Company would retake the hill followed by A Company, who would retake more territory surrounding the hill and allow F Company to withdraw back to the main line of resistance. Leading this mission would be Cronkhite of the F Company, 2nd Battalion and Lieutenant John Porterfield of the A Company, 1st Battalion.

But as the assault began, confusion and uncertainty occurred among the attacking companies. DeGavre told Betances Ramírez to keep F Company on the hill. Whether through mistake or miscommunication, Cronkhite had also received orders to hold the hill. It quickly became unclear which companies would be remaining on Hill 391 and which would be withdrawing.

Cronkhite and F Company drove the Chinese forces off Hill 391 and secured their objective by 9:55 a.m. But Cronkhite did not update Porterfield right away, expecting instead to see him soon as A Company passed through the outpost. Soon enemy fire was raining down on them once again. On the bare and rocky hill, they could barely defend themselves.

With such closely grouped troops from both A and F Companies, the constant enemy fire would cause more casualties. Around noon, the two company commanders met. Porterfield, the more experienced leader, decided that F Company would remain on the hill under Cronkhite and A Company would withdraw. But moments later, a mortar hit the two companies. Porterfield dropped to the ground, killed by enemy fire. Others in the group were killed or injured, but Cronkhite survived.

Confused and in shock, men from both companies retreated down the hill. Cronkhite scrambled to pull out his radio and informed Betances Ramírez that Porterfield was dead and that they could not hold the hill. Betances Ramírez directed him to stay on the hill and gave orders to send A Company back to the main line, leaving F Company to hold the hill on their own.

After Cronkhite disconnected with Betances Ramírez, he looked up. As he looked around at the barren and desolate rocky terrain, he only

Jackson Heights, or Hill 391, was a steep hill located close by to sites of other concurrent battles, including Hill 388 (*seen near the top of the image*).

saw one squad and a few officers among the living. Plumes of mortar smoke hung in the air. He realized that "all of Company A was gone. How many of them bugged out when their company commander got killed, how many of them carried [the wounded] back, I'll never know."

Former soldier Leonardo Justiniano from the A Company remembered, "[It] was a massacre. There were too many people wounded. Many dead. An avalanche of screaming."

At five in the afternoon, Cronkhite radioed Betances Ramírez to tell him that only ten soldiers remained on Hill 391. Again, he requested

Near Maejong, North Korea, soldiers from the 65th's 3rd Division help evacuate army photographer Robert H. Forsyth shortly after enemy fire wounded him while on patrol.

a withdrawal. It was refused. A few minutes later, the radio crackled with the voice of the H Company leader, who was holding a nearby hill. He reported that some of Cronkhite's men had gathered on his hill. He ordered the men to return to Hill 391. Most refused.

Betances Ramírez went to the men and spoke to them in Spanish, attempting to raise their morale. He reminded them they were the pride of Puerto Rico. When the soldiers continued to refuse, he told them desertion was a serious offense. He informed them of the possible consequences. The soldiers listened but did not change their minds. They were in shock.

Finally, Betances Ramírez went soldier by soldier and asked, "Are you returning?"

One by one, they answered. A handful said yes and were told to stand apart. But thirty-eight soldiers refused to return to Hill 391. Betances Ramírez ordered to disarm each of them and had them arrested. Meanwhile, Cronkhite decided to withdraw the few men left on the hill. They made it back down the hill to the main line of resistance.

On October 29, the 1st Battalion tried to recapture Hill 391. Under cover of fog, they secured the hill by 7:20 a.m. But the gruesome sight of the hill horrified the soldiers. The ground was covered with fallen soldiers from both sides. In shock, one of the platoon leaders looked around and realized his squad was gone. Walking back, he saw his men retreating down the hill. Confused, he stopped them and asked what they were doing. But the men responded in Spanish, and he could not understand them. The men continued down the hill.

By 10:50 a.m., fifty-eight men from 1st Battalion, C Company made their way back down the hill to the main line of resistance. They refused to return to Hill 391. When they arrived at the main line, they were disarmed and arrested. By afternoon, only thirteen men from the 1st Battalion remained on the hill. Fourteen men from A Company, seventy-six men from C Company, and thirty-two men from F Company were arrested for refusing their orders or misbehaving in front of the enemy.

During the last week of October, the 65th Infantry Regiment had 121 casualties. Early November was no better. The men still remembered the horrid scene and the screams of their fellow soldiers. Some of the men refused to fight. Many of these men were detained and had charges brought against them ranging from willfully disobeying orders to desertion. They were placed in a pen of barbed wire until they could be transported away from the front lines. One soldier remembered, "We went to see them. . . . Imagine when you don't know what's going to happen to you and they accuse you of something like that in the Army . . . of cowardice. And you are not a coward, you are a proven warrior. That will affect you for the rest of your life. They were very sad, it made you want to cry."

Most of the unit was pulled from the front line on October 29. From

> They accuse you of something like that in the Army . . . of cowardice. And you are not a coward, you are a proven warrior.

late October through late December, they were limited to conducting training exercises. Betances Ramírez was relieved of his duty by DeGavre. None of the officers from the continental US involved in the incidents were removed from duty.

A similar double standard appeared later that December when the 15th Infantry Division was ordered to retake Hill 391. The assault failed, and during the attack a patrol of US soldiers retreated and refused to return. None of those men were court-martialed after the retreat.

In late December, the unit was sent back to the front line, but this lasted only a week. In early January 1953, the entire 3rd Division, including the 65th Infantry Division, began a nine-week training program, which was briefly interrupted by a defense maneuver in late January. In January they had 2 battle casualties and 255 nonbattle-related casualties, mostly due to the freezing weather.

In late February 1953, the 65th Infantry Regiment began becoming a fully integrated unit. Most of the soldiers were moved to various other divisions, and new recruits were assigned to whichever regiments needed them, rather than to the 65th by default. And recruits from the continental US could be assigned to the 65th just like any other regiment. With these changes, the 65th Infantry Regiment was no longer a segregated Puerto Rican unit in the army. By June, after extensive training, they were back on the front lines again and fighting honorably.

After Eisenhower was elected, he went to Korea in November 1952. Eisenhower wanted to end the war. The static war plus the mounting casualties caused both the United States and China to want to end the war. Stalin died in March 1953. The new leaders of the Soviet Union were more concerned about economic problems than continuing the war in Korea. On July 27, 1953, the Korean War ended. At ten in the morning, China, North Korea, and the United States finally signed an armistice, or a truce. The cease-fire began at ten at night. South Korea refused to sign because they were seeking to reunify the North and the South. Today, there is still no peace treaty.

CHAPTER 10
Courts-Martial

The Puerto Ricans have proven in action in early fighting in Korea that they are a gallant people and that they will fight just as well as anyone else if they are properly trained and properly led.

—General J. Lawton Collins

O ver one hundred men from the 65th Infantry Regiment were arrested following the retreat from Hill 391. Ninety-six of them were court-martialed. The charges ranged from disobeying orders to avoiding combat to misbehaving. There were so many charged soldiers that the military divided them into fifteen trials. It was the largest court-martial of the Korean War.

Immediately after their arrest, the charged soldiers were thrust into the courtrooms. They had no time to call an attorney. As former soldier Angel L. Soler-Flores remembered, "I just sat in a chair and we went to it. They said I was a coward . . . the captain argued, how could a soldier who has removed two injured men in combat be a coward? So they reduced the sentence and gave me six months."

Sitting in a makeshift shelter while on reserve in May 1951, Private Francisco Jiminez O'Neill of Ciega, Puerto Rico, pens a letter to send home. Many Borinqueneers wrote to their families throughout the Korean War. It was through letters such as these that Puerto Ricans became aware of the unfair court-martial.

The speedy courts-martial barely lasted a month, ending by January 1953. According to the court transcripts, none of the men called on additional witnesses or offered evidence to support their case. As a form of protest, and in some cases from shock, "each of the accused, having been informed by the law officer of his rights as a witness in his own behalf, elected to remain silent." A few men had their charges dismissed, but ninety-one men were found guilty. The sentence: To be dishonorably discharged from the service, to forfeit all pay and allowances, and to be confined at hard labor. The length of the sentences ranged from six months to many years.

Meanwhile, Smythe commissioned a report on the 65th because he considered the unit "totally unfit for combat." He wanted the regiment either fully integrated, like other units in the army, or eliminated. The report concluded that the "failure of the 65th Infantry to retake JACKSON HEIGHTS was not due to enemy action, but rather to a disintegration in discipline and esprit de corps [pride and fellowship shared by members of a group]."

About half of the men sentenced had previously received report cards of excellent service before the retreat at Hill 391. Most of the other Borinqueneers had received ratings of good or satisfactory. Only one had previously stood military trial.

The army tried to keep the courts-martial quiet. They lied about the number of soldiers that stood trial. Initially, the 3rd Infantry Division announced that eighty-eight soldiers were tried by courts-martial and convicted. Two days later, on January 27, 1953, Smythe reported that ninety-two soldiers from the 65th were convicted.

In Puerto Rico the local press and political leaders, especially the governor, Luis Muñoz Marín, "promoted the ideals of heroism, democracy, freedom, and the war as a sort of rite of passage from which a new Puerto Rican man ready to build a modern Puerto Rico would emerge." They used the argument to push for a more independent government. And this call to arms from the government kept up the

'Deserter' Regiment Still
Tough, Hard-Fighting Outfit

Rec
Na
In S

65th's Record of Service Is Good

By PHIL NEWSOM
United Press Foreign News Editor

One of the worst things that can happen to a man, happened to 94 men on the U.S. Third Division's 65th Regiment.

They broke and ran before the enemy.

Yet those 94 men didn't make up the regiment. A regiment is about 5000 men.

And if's too bad that now, because of the publicity centered on the case, the whole 65th is suffering for the 94.

I remember the 65th.

'Stragglers, Yes, But Not Cowards'

WITH U.S. 2ND DIVISION, Korea, Jan. 29.—(AP)—The commanding general of the 2nd Division told today how he used frontline lectures to make good fighting men of more than 100 "stragglers" at the battle of Old Baldy hill.

Their return to battle spared them from courts martial.

Maj. Gen. James C. Fry said he was "shocked" last July 18 when told of the great number of men who had fled from the front.

"However," he said, "one thing stood clearly in my mind. Those men failed to fight as we thought

Puerto Rican Troops 'Bitter'

SAN JUAN, Puerto Rico, Jan. 29.—(AP)—Puerto Rican soldiers who were court-martialed for refusing to fight in Korea were bitter over lack of food, ammunition and long front line duty, one of their colleagues has charged in a letter home.

The charges were contained in a letter written by a private first class from Chorwon, Korea, on October 30, shortly after the

F
SEO
Nation
Land 1
village
prised
thing b

For
raiders
matic ·
ades, fi
charge
caught

From
and mo
the ra
upon th

"We
a fron

Newspapers across the country reported on the events of Outpost Kelly and Hill 391, most of them insulting or disparaging the soldiers of the 65th Infantry Regiment. Some articles, however, highlighted the regiment's historic achievements and overall good performance in combat.

steady stream of Puerto Rican soldiers enlisting in the military. When the news of the full extent of the courts-martial reached the governor of Puerto Rico, he and members of the Puerto Rican press requested an inquiry into the courts-martial.

The soldiers wrote letters to friends and family explaining what happened to them. A group of parents wrote a letter to Eisenhower asking for their sons, husbands, and uncles to be pardoned so they could fight and prove they were not cowards. Muñoz Marín demanded that a group of Puerto Rican lawyers be allowed to meet with the court-martialed soldiers.

In one article, the *New York Times* said,

> It was not the first time in war that troops had panicked under fire, but it was the first mass conviction by a courts martial for such action. It was also the first case in this war in which

men from a unit that had won international recognition for bravery unexplainedly seemed to have changed their character under fire.

The regiment fought in nine major Korean campaigns and its members had won 1,007 personal decorations including 162 Silver Stars and four Distinguished Service Crosses . . . the Sixty-fifth helped the marines as a rear guard during the bitter Hungnam evacuation, it was the first regiment to re-enter Seoul in 1951 and it was instrumental in breaking the "Iron Triangle" during the summer of 1951.

Secretary of the Army Robert Stevens had approved the original sentences. But because of pressure from the press, Congress, and the government of Puerto Rico, he changed his mind and granted clemency to fifty-three of the convicted men, reducing or clearing their sentences. By 1954 all ninety-one of the accused received clemency or full pardons. In the end, as stated by the Department of Defense, "All of the 65th Infantry Regiment veterans were given honorable discharges."

CHAPTER 11
The Legacy of the Borinqueneers

From World War I almost a century ago to Afghanistan today, American citizens from Puerto Rico have built and maintained a rich record of military service. If you visit any US military installation, you will see men and women from Puerto Rico, fighting to keep this nation safe, strong, and free.

—Pedro Pierluisi, governor of Puerto Rico

The story of the Borinqueneers has been largely forgotten, found mostly in army records. The Korean War is often called the Forgotten War because it is often overshadowed by World War II and the Vietnam War. But sixty years after the end of the Korean War, older Borinqueneers and the descendants of soldiers from the 65th Infantry Regiment began a grassroots effort to push the US Congress to award the 65th Infantry Regiment the Congressional Gold Medal, one of the highest civilian awards in the land. The Congressional Gold Medal is

From left to right, Sergeant Carmelo C. Mathews, Captain Francisco Orobitg, and Private Angel Perales hold up a Puerto Rican flag on the battlefield in Korea.

awarded by Congress as "its highest expression of national appreciation for distinguished achievements and contributions." Congress has issued fewer than two hundred of these medals in US history. But in 2014, the grassroots movement attained its goal. On June 10, 2014, President Barak Obama signed the bill that awarded the Congressional Gold Medal to the Borinqueneers. Obama spoke about the last segregated unit in the army:

> In World War I, they defended the homeland and patrolled the Panama Canal Zone. In World War II, they fought in

Europe. In Korea they fought in mud and snow. They are the 65th Infantry Regiment. . . . [Segregation] set them apart from their fellow soldiers—but their courage made them legendary.

On April 13, 2016, representatives of the 65th Infantry were presented with the Congressional Gold Medal on Capitol Hill. During the award ceremony, Speaker of the House Paul Ryan asked the audience, "Would you fight for a country who discriminated against you? . . . It takes a certain caliber of man to do that."

> [Segregation] set them apart from their fellow soldiers—but their courage made them legendary.

Many of the soldiers of the 65th Infantry Regiment were also honored for their bravery in the Korean War. But many people thought the awards were insufficient to properly recognize the valor of their actions. Cartagena's heroic actions at Hill 206, for instance, earned him the Distinguished Service Cross, the second-highest medal the military awards. This confused some, believing he deserved the highest medal, the Medal of Honor. His son Modesto Cartagena Jr. said, "When investigations began to award my dad a medal [and the recommendation package was put together], it was difficult to get written testimony because all of the unit were Puerto Rican and many of them had limited English proficiency. The officer in charge wrote one account and passed it around for all of the troops to read and sign, instead of getting more individual witnesses."

While many of the men of the 65th Infantry have died, it is still important that we remember their history and celebrate their contributions to the history of the US military. They must not become forgotten soldiers of the Forgotten War. Their story is the story of so many soldiers of color throughout the history of the US military. They fought valiantly and defended their fellow American soldiers even in

Sergeant Major Jose Colon (*middle left*) and Colonel Manuel Siverio Sr. (*middle right*) accept the Congressional Gold Medal on behalf of the 65th Infantry Regiment.

the face of prejudice, discrimination, and segregation from within the military. Their courage and loyalty left an imprint on the military in their own time, causing even the highest-ranking officers to acknowledge the impact of their service. Even today, we can see how the story of the Borinqueneers has inspired awe and appreciation from all those who pushed to have their deeds recognized by the US government. The story of the 65th Infantry Regiment will live on as proof of the bravery and sacrifice contributed by the soldiers of Puerto Rico.

TIMELINE OF THE 65TH INFANTRY REGIMENT

1493   **November 19**   Christopher Columbus lands in Borinquen (Puerto Rico) and encounters the Taíno people.

1898   The Treaty of Paris ends the Spanish-American War and gives the US control over Puerto Rico.

1908   Puerto Rico is temporarily renamed Porto Rico.

1910   Japan takes control over the Korean peninsula.

1915   **March 21**   The first shot is fired by the US against German forces in World War I when the Porto Rico Regiment of Infantry fires upon the German ship *Odenwald*.

1917   Puerto Ricans gain US citizenship.

1920   The Porto Rico Regiment of Infantry is integrated into the US military and renamed the 65th Infantry Regiment.

1932   Porto Rico is renamed Puerto Rico.

1941   **December 7**   The Japanese Empire conducts a surprise attack on Pearl Harbor, and the US enters World War II.

1944   **December**   The 65th Infantry Regiment engages in active combat for the first time.

1945   **May**   Germany surrenders, ending the war in Europe.

  September   Japan surrenders, ending World War II. The Korean peninsula is divided into North and South Korea.

1950	February	Organizing begins for Operation PORTREX, the largest military exercise to date.
	March	Operation PORTREX begins on the island of Vieques. The 65th Infantry Regiment successfully defends Vieques.
	June	The NKPA invades South Korea, capturing Seoul, South Korea.
	July	NKPA forces capture Incheon, South Korea.
	August	The 65th Infantry Regiment embarks for Korea and takes the nickname Borinqueneers.
	September	United Nations Command enacts a combined assault near Incheon led by the US military. The 65th Infantry Regiment lands in Pusan, South Korea.
	October	UNC forces recapture Seoul and push the NKPA north to the Yalu River. The PVA crosses the Yalu River into North Korea.
	December	The US Marines withdraw from the Chosin Reservoir.
	December 24	The evacuation of Hungham is completed, and the port is destroyed to prevent its use by NKPA and PVA forces.
1951	January	NKPA and PVA forces recapture Seoul. Lieutenant General Walker is killed in a jeep accident. Matthew Ridgway is promoted to lieutenant general of the 8th Army.
	March	UNC forces cross the Han River and recapture Seoul for the final time.
	April 11	General MacArthur is removed from command and replaced by Lieutenant General Matthew Ridgway.
	July 10	Armistice discussions begin in Kaesong.
	October	Armistice discussions are relocated to Panmunjom.

1952	September 18	PVA forces attack and take Outpost Kelly.
	October 25	PVA forces attack Hill 391 (Jackson Heights).
	October 27	The 65th Infantry Regiment withdraws from Hill 391.
	October 29	The 65th Infantry Regiment is ordered to retake Hill 391. Over one hundred soldiers are arrested for refusing orders.
	December	The 65th Infantry Regiment is removed from the front lines, the 15th Infantry Division is ordered to retake Hill 391, and many soldiers refuse to engage the enemy.
1953	January	The largest court-martial in the Korean War ends; ninety-one 65th Infantry soldiers are found guilty.
1953	July 27	The demilitarized zone is created along the 38th parallel. The Korean War ends.
1954		All ninety-one court-martialed soldiers of the 65th Infantry Regiment receive clemency or full pardons.
2016	April	The 65th Infantry Regiment receives the Congressional Gold Medal.

GLOSSARY

active duty: employment as a full-time member of the military

air raid: an attack by armed airplanes on a surface target

barrack: one or more buildings designated to house soldiers

barricade: an improved structure for defending one side of a battle against enemy attacks

basic training: the initial training of a military recruit

Communist: an advocate of a political and economic system that seeks to ensure all private property is collectively owned and managed

court-martial: a judicial court to try military service members accused of violating military law; the act of trying someone by a court-martial

draftee: a soldier conscripted for military service by the government

emplacement: a set location meant to place military weapons or equipment

executive order: in the US, a directive issued by the president to federal agencies

front line: the position or station closest to active, armed conflict

guerrilla unit: an informal military unit that typically fights using limited and unconventional tactics

honorable discharge: an official release from the military at the end of a person's service

maná: a usually sudden and unexpected source of pleasure or gain

mortar: a small, easily portable military weapon that fires explosive shells in high-arching, indirect ballistic trajectories

noncommissioned officer (NCO): a subordinate officer (such as a sergeant) in the army, air force, or marine corps appointed from among enlisted personnel

paratrooper: a soldier trained to parachute into military operations, typically as part of an airborne attack

patrol: a unit of persons or vehicles employed for reconnaissance, security, or combat

protectorate: the relationship of superior authority assumed by one power or state over a dependent one

reserve unit: a trained military force who are not committed to battle but remain available to deploy in the case of unexpected situations or opportunities

SOURCE NOTES

10 "brilliant record of heroism": Shannon Collins, "Congress Honors Puerto Rican Regiment for Heroic Korean War Service," U.S. Department of Defense, October 11, 2016, https://www.defense.gov /News/News-Stories/Article/Article/967929/congress-honors-puerto -rican-regiment-for-heroic-korean-war-service/.

11 "The 65th participated . . . as white soldiers.": *Puerto Rican Voices*, season 3, episode 7, "The Pride of Our People," Center for Puerto Rican Studies, Hunter College, 00:01:21–00:08:17, https://centropr -archive.hunter.cuny.edu/centro-tv/puerto-rican-voices/pr-voices-s3e7 -pride-our-people.

13 "father": Michael E. Haskew, *West Point 1915: Eisenhower, Bradley, and the Class the Stars Fell On* (Minneapolis: Zenith, 2014), 13, 37.

17 "That's how they . . . in the Army.": Noemí Figueroa Soulet, *The Borinqueneers*, directed by Noemí Figueroa Soulet and Raquel Ortiz (Kissimmee, FL: El Pozo Productions, 2007), DVD, 11:31.

21 "We arrived at . . . a tremendous welcome": Figueroa Soulet, 14:58.

22 "It is hereby . . . or national origin.": Exec. Order No. 9981 (July 26, 1948), Fed. Reg., 1–2, https://www.trumanlibrary.gov/library/research -files/executive-order-9981-desegregation-armed-forces.

24 "It was clearly . . . lose the battle.": W. W. Harris, *Puerto Rico's Fighting 65th U.S. Infantry: From San Juan to Chorwan* (San Rafael, CA: Presidio, 1980), 16.

24 "rum and Coca-Cola outfit": Harris, 1.

24 "had an immediate . . . revocation amazed [Harris].": Harris, 9, 14.

25 "a steady flow . . . to our headquarters.": Edwin L. Sibert, "Operation PORTREX," CIA, September 22, 1993, https://www.cia.gov /static/94f7873472061cfc5e6f381a8e5395d7/Operation-Portrex.pdf.

26 "Umpires judged that . . . been wiped out.": Hanson W. Baldwin, "D-Day on Vieques Finds Going Tough: Umpires Judge That in War Battalion Would Have Lost 50% in Casualties," *New York Times*, March 9, 1950.

26 "The invaders also . . . for a maneuver": Baldwin.

26 "We were supposed . . . us look bad.": Figueroa Soulet, *The Borinqueneers*, 18:31.

26 "Instead of knocking . . . completely impassable.": Harris, *Puerto Rico's Fighting 65th*, 25.

27 "There is not . . . defenders of Vieques.": Baldwin, "D-Day."

28 "Here's something for you": Hanson W. Baldwin, "Last Action Today in Caribbean 'War': 'Invaders' Land 16,000 Men on Island of Vieques—Seven Lost in the Maneuvers," *New York Times*, March 11, 1950.

28 "This is a . . . are now dead.": Harris, *Puerto Rico's Fighting 65th*, 31.

29 "Probably the greatest . . . someday pay off.": Hanson W. Baldwin, "Portrex May Bring Operating Changes—Technique of Amphibious and Joint Drills Faces Shift as a Result of Findings—Wide Satisfaction Voiced—But Small Land Mass Targets Are Viewed by Some Officers as Something of the Past," *New York Times*, March 14, 1950.

31 "After taking manpower . . . Korean War broke out.": Gilberto Villahermosa, *Honor and Fidelity: The 65th Infantry in Korea, 1950–1953* (Washington, DC: Center of Military History, United States Army, 2009), 13.

34 "We were humiliated . . . mere caretaking establishment.": Harris, *Puerto Rico's Fighting 65th*, 39.

34 "You and I . . . and the Pentagon": Harris, 42.

35 "You know . . . headed for Korea.": Harris, 43.

36 "You are directed . . . Infantry Regiment (secret).": Harris, 43.

36 "Question: Request 65th . . . to combat-load (secret).": Harris, 44.

36 "Negative.": Harris, 44.

37 "Question: Request authorization . . . of question (secret).": Harris, 45.

37 "Approved.": Harris, 45.

37–38 "As a youth . . . serve my country.": Nicolas Santiago-Rosario, Veterans History Project, December 11, 2002, 00:01:28, accessed November 4, 2022, https://memory.loc.gov/diglib/vhp/story/loc.natlib.afc2001001.24856/sr0001001.stream.

39 "We didn't know where we were going": Manuel Rivera-Santiago, interview by Coralina Rivera, July 27–30, 2004, Veterans History Project, Library of Congress, transcript, https://memory.loc.gov/diglib/vhp/story/loc.natlib.afc2001001.88481/transcript?ID=mv0001.

39 "The chow line . . . a real mess.": J. D. Leipold and C. Todd Lopez, "65th Infantry Regiment Receives Congressional Gold Medal," U.S. Army, April 15, 2016, https://www.army.mil/article/165991/65th _infantry_regiment_receives_congressional_gold_medal.

39 "Willy-nilly, our troops . . . dry-gulched our soldiers": Harris, *Puerto Rico's Fighting 65th*, 48–49.

43 "Do you see those trains?": Harris, 56.

43 "Get on them and go that way": Harris, 56.

45 "The 65th had . . . me with abandon.": Figueroa Soulet, *The Borinqueneers*, 25:10.

46 "The crash of . . . by a bullet.": Harris, *Puerto Rico's Fighting 65th*, 57.

47–48 "halted for the . . . as a barricade.": Harris, 58.

48 "cool, determined, self-reliant . . . effective combat soldiers.": Harris, 71.

50 "They must be some fighters": Harris, 89.

54 "From Harris to . . . period signed Harris.": Harris, 99.

54 "Maná del cielo!": Harris, 103.

54 "General Almond said . . . didn't trust them.": Harris, 104.

54 "have fought like real troopers.": Harris, 105.

59 "Happiness is being . . . of false security.": Harris, 94.

61 "We had so . . . layers of clothing": Celestino Cordova, interview with the author, January 21, 2018.

61 "The most we . . . Christmas-fed ducks": Harris, *Puerto Rico's Fighting 65th*, 134.

67 "We finally left . . . trip over them.": Rivera-Santiago, interview.

68 "One of the . . . 65th Infantry Regiment.": "Hungnam," *Charleston Gazette*, January 7, 1951.

71 "Self-reliance, stamina, courage . . . of the 65th.": Harris, *Puerto Rico's Fighting 65th*, 151.

72 "One of the . . . I was unconscious.": Harris, 150.

75 "un-American . . . accept leadership themselves.": Matthew B. Ridgway, *The Korean War* (New York: Da Capo, 1967), 193.

77 "What was that? . . . dead or captured.": Harris, *Puerto Rico's Fighting 65th*, 165–166.

78 "I am proud . . . over our enemies.": Harris, 168.

78 "to the men . . . principles of democracy.": Villahermosa, *Honor and Fidelity*, 95.

78 "walked up to . . . they have been?": Noemí Figueroa Soulet, *The Borinqueneers: A Visual History of the 65th Infantry Regiment* (Kissimmee, FL: El Pozo Productions, 2022), 104.

81 "The Puerto Ricans . . . heroism in battle.": Collins, "Congress Honors Puerto Rican Regiment."

83 "seesaw operations.": Harris, *Puerto Rico's Fighting 65th*, 179.

85 "battle exhaustion.": Villahermosa, *Honor and Fidelity*, 120.

85 "a soldier would . . . of the two.": Villahermosa, 121.

86 "a bit emotional": Harris, *Puerto Rico's Fighting 65th*, 197.

88 "The Hollywood style . . . from the hip.": Harris, 192.

89 "the shortage of . . . problem will arise.": Villahermosa, *Honor and Fidelity*, 160.

91 "The war changed . . . it became static.": Figueroa Soulet, *The Borinqueneers*, 37:45.

92 "gallant and effective . . . the military services.": Danny Nieves, "Master Sergeant Pedro J. Zayas," valerosos.com, September 22, 2021, http://www.valerosos.com/MstSgtPedroJZayas.html.

94 "during the first . . . and gained 3,825.": Villahermosa, *Honor and Fidelity*, 205.

94 "3rd Infantry Division": Villahermosa, 185.

95 "The inability to . . . misinterpretation or misunderstanding.": Villahermosa, 214.

97–98 "There was a . . . our own troops.": Villahermosa, 222.

98 "It looked . . . very traumatic experience.": Figueroa Soulet, *The Borinqueneers*, 46:11.

98 "Thirty-eight men went up. Three came down.": Matthew Hay Brown, "New Generation Fights for 65th," *Orlando Sentinel*, May 26, 2002, https://www.orlandosentinel.com/news/os-xpm-2002-05-27 -0205270238-story.html.

100 "When I came . . . It's just unbelievable.": Figueroa Soulet, *The Borinqueneers*, 46:11.

101 "Until such a . . . of their manhood": Brown, "New Generation Fights for 65th."

101 "It is part . . . its importance, unsuccessfully.": Brown.

102 "It was a . . . we had none.": Figueroa Soulet, *The Borinqueneers*, 86.

102 "needed more time . . . duties of NCOs.": Figueroa Soulet, 242.

103 "rounds . . . from every direction": Figueroa Soulet, 54:01.

103 "It was horrible . . . It was everywhere": Figueroa Soulet, 53:58.

105 "all of Company . . . I'll never know.": Villahermosa, *Honor and Fidelity*, 256–257.

105 "[It] was a . . . avalanche of screaming.": Figueroa Soulet, *The Borinqueneers*, 56:03.

106 "Are you returning?": Figueroa Soulet, 57:55.

107 "We went to . . . want to cry.": Figueroa Soulet, 01:01:30.

109 "The Puerto Ricans . . . and properly led.": Brown, "New Generation Fights for 65th."

109 "I just sad . . . me six months.": Figueroa Soulet, *The Borinqueneers*, 01:02:29.

111 "each of the . . . to remain silent.": United States v. Private First Class Victor Gonzalez-Marquez (US29136485), Private First Class Sergio Lopez-Lopez (US 50112294), Private First Class Antonio I. Mignucci (US 50106763), Private First Class Amador Negron-Sanchez (US 50110005), Private First Class Jesus Nieves-Crespo (US 50109646), Private Guiellermo Ortiz-Colon (US 29155239), Private First Class Bartolo Ramos-Diaz (US 50110531), Private First Class Severiano Santiago-Rodriquez (US 50109747), Private First Class Felix Santiago-Santana (US 50108621), and Prvaite First Class Pelegrin Valdes-Fernandez (US 50109857), all of Company L, 65 Infantry Regiment, APO 468, CM 360543 (7 December, 1952).

111 "totally unfit for combat.": Villahermosa, *Honor and Fidelity*, 271.

111 "failure of the . . . of a group].": Villahermosa, 261.

111 "promoted the ideals . . . Rico would emerge.": Harry Franqui-Rivera, "Borinqueneers Day and the Korean War in Puerto Rican History and Memory," Center for Puerto Rican Studies, April 12, 2021, https://centropr-archive.hunter.cuny.edu/centrovoices/chronicles /borinqueneers-day-and-korean-war-puerto-rican-history-and-memory.

112–113   "It was not . . . summer of 1951.": Greg MacGregor, "Army Tells Story of Troops Who Ran—Panic in Puerto Rican Regiment in Korea Confined to 92—General Lauds Others," *New York Times*, January 28, 1953.

113   "All of the . . . given honorable discharges.": Collins, "Congress Honors Puerto Rican Regiment."

114   "For generations, from . . . strong, and free.": "Obama Awards Borinqueneers with Congressional Gold Medal," NBC News, June 10, 2014, https://www.nbcnews.com/news/latino/obama-awards -borinqueneers-congressional-gold-medal-n127451.

115   "its highest expression . . . achievements and contributions.": "Congressional Gold Medal Recipients," U.S. House of Representatives, accessed September 12, 2022, https://history .house.gov/Institution/Gold-Medal/Gold-Medal-Recipients/.

115–116   "In World War . . . made them legendary.": The White House Office of the Press Secretary, "Remarks by the President at Signing of the Water Resources Reform and Development Act and the 65th Infantry Regiment Congressional Gold Medal," press release, June 10, 2014, https://obamawhitehouse.archives.gov/the-press -office/2014/06/10/remarks-president-signing-water-resources -reform-and-development-act-and.

116   "Would you fight . . . to do that.": The Office of Corporate Communications, "The Congressional Gold Medal Awarded to the 65th Regiment, the Borinqueneers," United States Mint, May 18, 2016, https://www.usmint.gov/news/inside-the-mint/congressional -gold-medal-awarded-to-65th-regiment-borinqueneers.

116   "When investigations began . . . more individual witnesses.": Ken Flynn, "Family Seeks Medal of Honor for Army Hero," *El Paso Times*, April 2002.

SELECTED BIBLIOGRAPHY

Booker, Herbert. *PORTREX Observers Handbook*. Available online at Internet Archive. Accessed December 19, 2016. https://archive.org/details/1950Portrex.

Borinqueneers Congressional Gold Medal Alliance. Accessed November 21, 2016. http://www.65thcgm.org/.

Brown, Matthew Hay. "Clearing the Borinqueneers." *Hartford (CT) Courant*, May 26, 2002. https://www.courant.com/news/connecticut/hc-xpm-2002-05 -26-0205260110-story.html.

Bruce, Mary. "Obama Awards Medal of Honor to 24 Vets Who Suffered Bias." ABC News, March 18, 2014. https://abcnews.go.com/blogs/politics /2014/03/obama-awards-medal-of-honor-to-24-vets-who-suffered-bias/.

Canales, Angel. "A Soldier's Mission to Honor Segregated 65th Regiment 'Borinqueneers.'" ABC News, June 13, 2014. http://abcnews.go.com/blogs /headlines/2014/06/a-soldiers-mission-to-honor-segregated-65th-regiment -borinqueneers/.

Collins, Shannon. "Congress Honors Puerto Rican Regiment for Heroic Korean War Service." U.S. Army, October 11, 2016. https://www.army.mil /article/176494/congress_honors_puerto_rican_regiment_for_heroic_korean _war_service.

———. "Puerto Ricans Represented throughout U.S. Military History." US Department of Defense, October 14, 2016. http://www.defense.gov/News /Article/Article/974518/puerto-ricans-represented-throughout-us-military -history.

Figueroa Soulet, Noemí. *The Borinqueneers*. Directed by Noemí Figueroa Soulet and Raquel Ortiz. Kissimmee, FL: El Pozo Productions, 2007.

Haskew, Michael. *West Point 1915: Eisenhower, Bradley, and the Class the Stars Fell On*. Minneapolis: Zenith, 2014.

"Hispanics in the U.S. Army." U.S. Army. Accessed September 21, 2016. https://www.army.mil/hispanics/history.html.

"Hungnam." *Charleston Gazette*, January 7, 1951.

"Puerto Ricans Devise Unique Heat Gadgets." *Stars and Stripes* (Pacific ed), December 1951.

"Puerto Rico—History and Heritage." *Smithsonian*, November 6, 2007. https://www.smithsonianmag.com/travel/puerto-rico-history-and-heritage -13990189/.

Ridgway, Matthew B. *The Korean War*. New York: Da Capo, 1967.

"65th Puerto Rican Reg't Gets New CO." *Stars and Stripes* (Pacific ed.), February 1952.

Stewart, Richard W. *Staff Operations: The X Corps in Korea, December 1950*. Fort Leavenworth, KS: Combat Studies Institute, 1991.

"Taino Indian Culture." Welcome to Puerto Rico. Accessed January 2, 2022. http://www.topuertorico.org/reference/taino.shtml.

To Award a Congressional Gold Medal to the 65th Infantry Regiment, Known as the Borinqueneers. H.R. 1726, 133rd Cong. (2014). https://www .gpo.gov/fdsys/pkg/PLAW-113publ120/html/PLAW-113publ120.htm.

Veterans History Project. Library of Congress. Accessed November 21, 2016. https://www.loc.gov/vets/.

Voces Oral History Center, Moody College of Communication, University of Texas at Austin. Accessed November 21, 2016. http://www.lib.utexas.edu /voces/.

Warner, Karl. "Combating Cold Korea." U.S. Army, November 10, 2010. https://army.togetherweserved.com/army/servlet/tws.webapp.WebApp?cmd =ShadowBoxProfile&type=Person&ID=357865.

"World War II Timeline–Scholastic." Girls Talk Math. Accessed January 1, 2018. http://gtm.math.umd.edu/lectures_2018/Scholastic_WW2_Timeline .pdf.

FURTHER INFORMATION

Books

Fuentes, Gabriel. *Return to Avalon*. Puerta Real, PR: Isleta, 2008.
Author Gabriel Fuentes tells the story of his father, Gabriel Fuentes Jr., a soldier in the 65th Infantry Regiment who served during World War II, highlighting the bravery of the Puerto Rican regiment.

Halberstam, David. *The Coldest Winter: America and the Korean War*. New York: Hachette Books, 2008.
Halberstam provides a detailed account of the main historical figures and political context of the Korean War.

Harris, William W. *Puerto Rico's Fighting 65th U.S. Infantry: From San Juan to Chorwan*. Novato, CA: Presidio, 2001.
Read Colonel Harris's own words in this detailed chronological story of his time serving as the leader of the 65th Infantry Regiment, from Operation PORTREX to his rotation out of Korea.

Seth, Shaun. *Key Figures of the Korean War*. Chicago: Britannica, 2015.
Gain a deeper understanding of the people and events surrounding the Korean War.

Villahermosa, Gilberto N. *Honor and Fidelity: The 65th Infantry in Korea, 1950–1953*. Washington DC: Center of Military History, 2009.
Author Villahermosa explains how the 65th Infantry Regiment formed and was able to perform well in combat despite their marginalization within the US Army, providing insight into how the army's interests affected the soldiers of the 65th.

Websites

"Bloodied in Battle, Now Getting Their Due"
https://www.nytimes.com/2007/10/02/nyregion/02vets.html
The writer of this *New York Times* article interviews multiple veterans of the 65th Infantry Regiment.

The Borinqueneers Gallery
https://borinqueneers.com/
This resource has photographs, audio, and film about the soldiers of the 65th Regiment throughout their entire history—before, during, and after the Korean War.

Centro Voices
https://centropr-archive.hunter.cuny.edu/centro-voices-newsletter
This online journal publishes articles on Puerto Rican current events and history and contains articles about Puerto Ricans' contributions to the Korean War.

"U.S. Navy Operation PORTREX 1950 Puerto Rico Landing Exercise 81164"
https://youtu.be/5iNxVgDAXZg
A short documentary from 1950, it details the timeline and tactics used during the Operation PORTREX exercise. Narration accompanies the film of the events, making it a quality primary source.

INDEX

ACKNOWLEDGMENTS

I would like to thank my husband for love, support, and encouragement as I wrote, edited, and re-edited this book. Thank you for reading drafts, keeping the little ones busy so I could write, and being the best cheerleader a person could ask for.

Thank you to my parents for all the babysitting hours to give me time to work on the book.

Thank you to the Lerner team! A special thank you to Shaina Olmanson for being so patient, honest, and kind; Lindsay Matvick and Megan Ciskowski for answering my numerous questions; Cole Nelson for such great feedback and support.

Thank you to Don Mounts, Balún, Celestino Cordova, and the other Borinqueneers who allowed me to interview them.

Thank you to the Center for Puerto Rican Studies at Hunter College and the Veterans History Project for providing me with rich content without it this project could not have happened.

ABOUT THE AUTHOR

Talia Aikens-Nuñez is passionate about sharing with young readers the little-known stories, accomplishments, and contributions of people of color from all throughout history. Aikens-Nuñez is the author of *Small Nap, Little Dream*, a bilingual Spanish/English picture book. She and her husband live on a river in Connecticut with their two children.

PHOTO ACKNOWLEDGMENTS

Image credits: National Archives (6519407), p. 9; Porto Rico Regiment/ Wikipedia (Public Domain), p. 14; U.S. Army Photo, pp. 19 (top) (bottom), 47, 53, 60, 61, 64, 72 (bottom), 87, 89, 96, 100, 105; Photo12/UIG/Getty Images, p. 20; Aviation History Collection/Alamy, pp. 27, 29; Archive Image/Alamy, pp. 33, 106; Universal Images Group/Getty Images, p. 34; National Guard, p. 38; Ruiz/National Archives, p. 41; Bettmann/Getty Images, pp. 42–43; colaimages/Alamy, p. 51 (top); Keystone/Getty Images, p. 51 (bottom); Everett Collection Historical/Alamy, p. 55; National Archives, pp. 56, 84, 110; SIPA Asia/ZUMA Wire/Alamy, p. 66; U.S. Navy Photo/Wikipedia (Public Domain), p. 69; American Photo Archive/Alamy, p. 73 (top); Robert Schutz/AP Photo, p. 76 (top); Photo by U.S. Army Photograph/Alamy, p. 76 (bottom); Archive Photos/Getty Images, p. 79; Max Desfor/AP Photo, p. 82; Science History Images/Alamy, p. 93; Robert Schutz/AP Photo, p. 99; Library of Congress, p. 112; AP Photo, p. 115; AP Photo/Manuel Balce Ceneta, p. 117.